"WHAT'S THE NUMBER FOR 9 1 1 ?"

"WHAT'S THE NUMBER FOR 911?"

AMERICA'S WACKIEST 911 CALLS

Leland H. Gregory III

Andrews McMeel Publishing

Kansas City

00 01 02 03 04 RDC 10 9 8 7 6 5 4 3 2 1

   Library of Congress Cataloging-in-Publication Data
Gregory, Leland.
   What's the number for 911? : America's wackiest 911 calls /
Leland Gregory.
      p.   cm.
   ISBN 0-7407-0032-4 (paperback)
   1. Emergency management—United States Anecdotes. 2. Crisis
management—United States Anecdotes. 3. Telephone—United
States—Emergency reporting systems Anecdotes. 4. Emergency
communication systems—United States Anecdotes. I. Title.
II. Title: What's the number for nine one one.
HV551.3.G74 2000
384.6'4—dc21   99-40324
                                                   CIP

Book design by Holly Camerlink

This book is dedicated to my wife,
Gloria Graves Gregory.
She's the one who took my 911 call
for help more than eleven years ago
and didn't put me on hold.
Thank you for everything!

ACKNOWLEDGMENTS

The author would first of all like to acknowledge the hard work and dedication of the men and women of the 911 system. They've taken their fair share of knocks in the media, but that's mainly because they are overburdened with the stupidity and silliness that you'll read about throughout this book. Of special note are the contributions and encouragement of J. H. Ronan, dispatcher, Virginia; John P. Yeast, communications manager, St. Louis, Missouri; John Burruss, NREMT-P Charlottesville-Albemarle Rescue Squad; and Virginia and Jerry Zezima of *Newsday*.

The first telephone call was a call for help. On March 10, 1876, Alexander Graham Bell was about to try a new transmitter and accidentally spilled battery acid on his clothes. Bell's assistant, Thomas A. Watson, was in the next room when he heard Bell's voice over the transmitter: "Mr. Watson, come here. I want you!"

It was some sixty years later, in 1937, before a centralized emergency number was utilized. Great Britain installed "999," which would reach a central operator who would then transfer the call.

Other countries have adopted similar systems: Belgium has "900," Denmark and Australia adopted "000," Sweden uses "80 000," and Japan has implemented "119." In the United States the first 911 call was placed on February 16, 1968, in Haleyville, Alabama.

So after Alexander Graham Bell's immortal call, it makes perfect sense that the telephone would become the instrument to help people in distress and that it would only be used responsibly, right? Well . . .

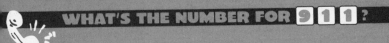

SICKENINGLY SUITE

DISPATCHER: "911. What is your emergency?"

FEMALE CALLER: "Yes, we just got to our hotel room and there are four of us here, but we only have enough towels for two."

DISPATCHER: "This is 911, ma'am."

CALLER: "Yes, well, what am I supposed to do?"

DISPATCHER: "Have you tried the hotel operator?"

THREE SHOTS AND YOU'RE OUT

A thirty-eight-year-old man from Princeton, West Virginia, made an emergency 911 call in October 1992 to complain about gunshot wounds—three of them. Paramedics arrived and discovered the man had accidentally shot himself three times in the right foot—each time with a different gun he was cleaning. According to Sheriff's Deputy L.R. Catron, the man claimed the first shot from the .32-caliber handgun he was cleaning didn't hurt so he went on to clean the second gun, a .38-caliber pistol. When that one went off and shot him in the foot, it "stung a little, but not too bad." However, it was only when his third gun, a .357, fired and hit him in the foot that he decided to call 911. The man stated the third one "really hurt because the bullet was a hollow point." Just in case you were wondering . . . yes, the man had been drinking at the time. Makes sense—beer and shots.

911 REPORT

"Please connect me to Switzerland."

LONG LIVE THE KING

911 DISPATCHER: "911. Fire or emergency?"

CALLER: "Oh, I would have to say emergency."

911 DISPATCHER: "What's the problem, ma'am?"

CALLER: "There's a fight going on. It's . . . down there. . . . I can see them through my window. They're in the parking lot. Oh, there's lots of yelling. They're cursing, too."

911 DISPATCHER: "Can you describe who's fighting please?"

CALLER: "I'll try. There's one man, and he's dressed like Elvis Presley. He's kicking another man who's laying on the ground and screaming 'You ain't nothing but a hound dog.'"

A CHAPLAINESQUE WEDDING

The wedding was scheduled for 1 P.M. on April 1, 1995. Jerry James Palmisano and his bride-to-be, Janice Smith, waited for their preacher—but he never showed up. By the time 3:30 rolled around, most of the guests had left, Smith had accidentally ripped her wedding gown, and Palmisano had broken the heel off his dress shoe. This was turning into a wedding emergency. So Palmisano went to a pay phone and dialed 911. While he was at the phone, a speeding car came by and splashed mud all over his tuxedo. "You've got to help me," he told Fort Pierce, Florida, police dispatchers. "It's the first 911 dispatch that I've responded to for a wedding," said the Reverend Charlie Wharton. "I made them call him back to make sure it wasn't a prank." Wharton, the Fort Pierce police chaplain, was dispatched to the Knights of Columbus hall, the scene of the wounded wedding. The family broke into "Here Comes the Bride" as Janice Smith, torn dress and all, walked down the aisle and married the man with mud on his tux. "Maybe this is all the bad things that are ever going to happen," Wharton said. Makes you wonder what their wedding night was like, doesn't it?

911 REPORT . . . 911 REPORT . . . 911 REPORT
. . . 911 REPORT . . . 911 REPORT . . . 911
RT . . . 911 REPORT . . . 911 REPORT . .
. . 911 REPORT . . . 911 REPORT . . . 911
911 REPORT . . . 911 REPORT . . . 911 REPORT
. 911 REPORT . . . 911 REPORT . . . 911
911 REPORT . . . 911 REPORT . . . 911 REPORT
. 911 REPORT . . . 911 REPORT . . . 911
911 REPORT "I have the hiccups." 911 REPORT
. 911 REPORT . . . 911 REPORT . . . 911
911 REPORT . . . 911 REPORT . . . 911 REPORT
. 911 REPORT . . . 911 REPORT . . . 911
911 REPORT . . . 911 REPORT . . . 911 REPORT
. 911 REPORT . . . 911 REPORT . . . 911
911 REPORT . . . 911 REPORT . . . 911 REPORT
. 911 REPORT . . . 911 REPORT . . . 911

6

911 REPORT . . . 911 REPORT . . . 911 REPORT

GUILTY BEFORE PROVEN GUILTY

911: "South Valley Dispatch."

BURGLAR: "Yeah hi, um, I just broke into a building. I'm inside the building right now, and I just got frustrated. I'm really upset right now. All I did was break the window, and I walked away, and I felt really guilty about it."

911: "Do you know what the name of it is, or anything like that?"

BURGLAR: "I could go look really quick if you want to hold on a minute."

911: "Okay. Will you come back?"

BURGLAR: "Yeah, I will."

911: "Okay."

BURGLAR: "Hold on a second. Now I'm gonna put the phone down."

911: "All right, put your hand in the air and walk out there."

BURGLAR: "Okay. I'm doing it right now."

911: "Okay, good."

BURGLAR: "Okay, bye."

911: "Bye."

IN AND OUTIE

A call came into the 911 center, and paramedics were immediately on their way to an "abdominal evisceration." The paramedics suited up in high-risk gloves, face shields, and other emergency gear in order to keep themselves safe. When they arrived at the residence, they found a thirteen-year-old boy lying on the bed motionless. They quickly examined the boy looking for a wound but couldn't find anything wrong. When they asked the boy why he had called 911, he told them because he had "stuff" coming out of his navel. Further investigation revealed the "stuff" to be belly-button lint.

911 REPORT ... 911 REPORT ... 911 REPORT
... 911 REPORT ... 911 REPORT ... 911
911 REPORT ... 911 REPORT ... 911 REPORT
... 911 REPORT ... 911 REPORT ... 911
911 REPORT ... 911 REPORT ... 911 REPORT
... 911 REPORT ... 911 REPORT ... 911

Male complainant called and
requested police call gas
stations on all exits I-95 to find
out which ones are open.

... 911 REPORT ... 911 REPORT ... 911
911 REPORT ... 911 REPORT ... 911 REPORT
... 911 REPORT ... 911 REPORT ... 911
911 REPORT ... 911 REPORT ... 911 REPORT
... 911 REPORT ... 911 REPORT ... 911

9

911 REPORT ... 911 REPORT ... 911 REPORT

REACH OUT AND TOUCH SOMEONE

In March 1996, Roy Holloway was at his preliminary hearing in Las Vegas on charges of attempted murder. During the attack on his wife, Holloway, frustrated over his inability to murder her, called 911 to complain. The call was played by the prosecution.

HOLLOWAY: "I've tried to strangle her about four different ways. She won't die."

OPERATOR: "Why are you trying to kill her?"

HOLLOWAY: "Because I don't like her."

OPERATOR: "Why not just divorce her?"

HOLLOWAY: "Isn't it a lot easier just to kill her? But she won't die. [G]od, she keeps breathing."

It's a lucky thing for Mrs. Holloway that Roy didn't accidentally get the prerecorded message that says "Please hang up and try again."

I SMELL A RAT

DISPATCHER: "911. What is your emergency?"

**TERRIFIED
FEMALE CALLER:** "Yes, I'd like to report a wild animal in my house."

DISPATCHER: "Yes."

CALLER: "It's wild. It's a mouse."

DISPATCHER: "I'm sorry, ma'am. You said it was a mouse?"

CALLER: "Yes! Yes! That's what I said. A mouse."

PILLOW TALK

"I was expecting the worst," said police communications unit director Frieda Lehner about a suicide call she received several years ago. The depressed man called the Albuquerque police headquarters, and Lehner engaged him in a conversation trying to talk the man out of any rash moves. They discussed his divorce and custody battle, his tour in Vietnam, and how he finally wound up living with his mother because he was unable to get a job even though he had looked. Lehner recalled that the man grew more and more agitated about how rotten his life had become. Suddenly, and to her horror, she heard a gunshot over the phone line. Then Lehner heard the phone drop—and then there was silence.

Soon she could hear the rustling of the phone being picked back up. "He came back on the line and he was extremely upset. He was using some very good adjectives. I was saying 'Are you hurt?' He said, 'I just shot my mother's favorite pillow. She's going to kill me.' That one was very stressful, but it turned out real good."

911 REPORT ... 911 REPORT ... 911 REPO
... 911 REPORT ... 911 REPORT ... 911
911 REPORT ... 911 REPORT ... 911 REPO
... 911 REPORT ... 911 REPORT ... 911
911 REPORT ... 911 REPORT ... 911 REPO
... 911 REPORT ... 911 REPORT ... 911
911 REPORT ... 911 REPORT ... 911 REPO
... 911 REPORT ... 911 REPORT ... 911

"My parrot got out and is
in a tree outside."

911 REPORT ... 911 REPORT ... 911 REPO
... 911 REPORT ... 911 REPORT ... 911
911 REPORT ... 911 REPORT ... 911 REPO
... 911 REPORT ... 911 REPORT ... 911
911 REPORT ... 911 REPORT ... 911 REPO
... 911 REPORT ... 911 REPORT ... 911
911 REPORT ... 911 REPORT ... 911 REPO

13

CHECK, PLEASE

DISPATCHER: "911. What's your emergency?"

MAN: "Well, let me tell you. My girlfriend, Sue, and I have been together for about three years now, see?"

DISPATCHER: "Yes."

MAN: "It's been great, too. No, really, I mean it. But recently, you know how it is, I mean, it's been like, well, things haven't been, well . . . we've been having some problems, you know."

DISPATCHER: "Sir."

MAN: "I'm getting there, I'm getting there. So, anyway, I really love her, man, it's just that, well, I think she's been . . . I think she is . . . well, you know, going out."

DISPATCHER: "Going out?"

MAN: "Yeah, you know, cheating on me, like."

DISPATCHER: "Sir, do you have an emergency?"

MAN: "I'm getting there, I'm getting there. So we had this big fight, you see . . . big one, too. So for the last couple of days I've been trying to call her . . . on the phone, right. No answer. Every time. No answer. I keep trying and stuff, but she don't answer the phone. I think she's cheating on me too. I'm sure she's home. It's not like she's in trouble or anything like that. It's just, well, I can't get in touch, and she won't answer the phone."

DISPATCHER: "Sir, I'm not sure how we can help you."

MAN: "Here's the thing. Why I called, see. I was hoping, you know, well, it's like, if you could send a cop by to see if she's home. And while they're there see what cars are parked in her driveway and maybe write down their license numbers and stuff. Since you guys can do stuff like that, you can find out who the cars belong to, right? Find out if she's there and who's there with her and stuff. I think she's cheating on me, but I don't have no proof . . . so, could you do that, you think?"

DISPATCHER: "Sir, this number is for emergency calls only. I'm sorry, but we can't help you."

MAN: "Sh-t!"

BOY, THAT SUCKED!

Lakeland, Florida, police and paramedics were dispatched on an early-morning 911 emergency made by a clerk at the Scottish Inn motel. The clerk called at 4:45 A.M. and pleaded with the operator to help a man who was stuck in the swimming pool. When they arrived on the scene, they quickly ascertained the problem. A man had his penis caught in the suction fitting of the motel's swimming pool.

"As I approached the man," went an officer's report, "I could see his pants were down to his knees and his penis was stuck in a suction hole located in the northside wall of the swimming pool."

Even though the pool's pump had been shut off before the police arrived, the man's penis had swollen to such a degree that he couldn't remove it from the suction hole. Paramedics squeezed a lubricant into and around the suction fitting and were finally able to "free willy" after about forty minutes. I'll bet the man was so sore after his little mishap he won't be doing the back stroke for a long time.

REPORT . . . 911 REPORT . . . 911 REPO
. 911 REPORT . . . 911 REPORT . . . 911
REPORT . . . 911 REPORT . . . 911 REPO
. 911 REPORT . . . 911 REPORT . . . 911
REPORT . . . 911 REPORT . . . 911 REPO
. 911 REPORT . . . 911 REPORT . . . 911
REPORT . . . 911 REPORT . . . 911 REPO
911 REPORT . . . 911 REPORT . . . 911

"I've got a roach stuck
in my ear."

REPORT . . . 911 REPORT . . . 911 REPO
911 REPORT . . . 911 REPORT . . . 911
REPORT . . . 911 REPORT . . . 911 REPO
911 REPORT . . . 911 REPORT . . . 911
REPORT . . . 911 REPORT . . . 911 REPO
911 REPORT . . . 911 REPORT . . . 911
REPORT . . . 911 REPORT . . . 911 REPO

17

A PHONE BUG

DISPATCHER: "Sheriff's Department."

MALE CALLER: "Yeah, I have an ant in my ear, and I tried to flush it out with water, but that only made it go in further . . . What should I do? It's buggin' the hell out of my eardrum."

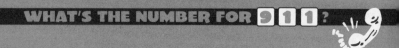

A REAL DOPE

DISPATCHER: "Sheriff's Department."

MALE CALLER: "Yeah, do you deliver dope? . . . Ahh, me and my girlfriend, we need some dope."

DISPATCHER: "Sir, this is the Sheriff's Department."

(Click.)

DISPATCHER: "Hello. Hello."

A SHOOTING PAIN

Gail Murphy dialed 911 after firing a shotgun through the front door of her house. Was she shooting at a burglar? the dispatcher asked. No, you see, Gail, who was recovering from hemorrhoid surgery, was angered at her husband's decision to go fishing with his buddies and not stay home and nurse her to health. Bad move. Even though Gail was forced to remain in bed on her stomach after the surgery, she was able to level the shotgun at the door when she heard her husband Edward returning home six hours later. Seems like Edward had been a pain in her rear longer than the hemorrhoids. He died of his wounds a few days later.

REPORT . . . 911 REPORT . . . 911 REPC
911 REPORT . . . 911 REPORT . . . 911
REPORT . . . 911 REPORT . . . 911 REPC
911 REPORT . . . 911 REPORT . . . 911
REPORT . . . 911 REPORT . . . 911 REPC
911 REPORT . . . 911 REPORT . . . 911
REPORT . . . 911 REPORT . . . 911 REPO

911 REPORT . . . 911 REPORT . . . 911
"When is the Cinco de Mayo
[Fifth of May] celebration?"

REPORT . . . 911 REPORT . . . 911 REPO
911 REPORT . . . 911 REPORT . . . 911
REPORT . . . 911 REPORT . . . 911 REPO
911 REPORT . . . 911 REPORT . . . 911
REPORT . . . 911 REPORT . . . 911 REPO
911 REPORT . . . 911 REPORT . . . 911
REPORT . . . 911 REPORT . . . 911 REPO

A FRIEND IN NEED . . .

MAN: "Yeah, hi. This is 678 Racine. And, um, I was called over to the residence. I think there's been a shooting here."

DISPATCHER: "OK, do you see a victim?"

MAN: "Yes."

DISPATCHER: "OK. Hold on for the paramedics, OK? One moment."

MAN: "OK."

DISPATCHER: "I want you to stay on the line."

MAN: "OK."

FIRE DISPATCHER: "Fire Department emergency operator. How may I help you?"

MAN: "Yeah, hi, there's been a shooting at Racine."

FIRE DISPATCHER: "How many people are shot?"

MAN: "Just one, and um . . . "

FIRE DISPATCHER: "Do you know what part of the body?"

MAN: "I think around the head and the neck. I just got here."

FIRE DISPATCHER: "The person who shot him, is he still around?"

MAN: "Yeah, she's his wife."

FIRE DISPATCHER: "*[unintelligible]* the wife shot him and they're both there?"

MAN: "Yeah."

FIRE DISPATCHER: "Is she hurt at all?"

MAN: "I'm not sure. I'm trying to calm her down. OK?"

POLICE DISPATCHER: "Hello, sir?"

MAN: "Yeah."

DISPATCHER: "Did, uh, was this on purpose, or was this an accident or what sir? Do you know what happened?"

MAN: "I have no idea. . . . She was drunk. She said she killed her husband, and I didn't believe her."

DISPATCHER: "OK, are they both there right now?"

MAN: "You're right. Now, can you trace this address because I'm not sure?"

DISPATCHER: "All right, where's the weapon now?"

MAN: "It's in my hand because, um, she brought it to my house."

DISPATCHER: "What's your name sir?"

MAN: "My name's Ron, Man."

DISPATCHER: "All right sir, we're going to get the officers on the way."

MAN: "OK."

REPORT . . . 911 REPORT . . . 911 REPO
911 REPORT . . . 911 REPORT . . . 911
REPORT . . . 911 REPORT . . . 911 REPO
911 REPORT . . . 911 REPORT . . . 911
REPORT . . . 911 REPORT . . . 911 REPO
911 REPORT . . . 911 REPORT . . . 911

Female complainant called
to request police officer
come to residence to change
battery in smoke detector
as she couldn't reach it.

911 REPORT . . . 911 REPORT . . . 911
REPORT . . . 911 REPORT . . . 911 REPO
911 REPORT . . . 911 REPORT . . . 911
REPORT . . . 911 REPORT . . . 911 REPO
911 REPORT . . . 911 REPORT . . . 911
REPORT . . . 911 REPORT . . . 911 REPO

THIS GUY WAS REALLY NUTS

It was a hostage situation. Seattle, Washington, police officer Steve Oskierko was the first on the scene—summoned by an emergency 911 phone call. He peered in through the glass doors of the John L. Scott real estate office and spotted the hostages. There were more than fifty office workers trembling in fear as the enraged hostage-taker paced menacingly in front of them. The hostages were in the back of the building—some holding boxes, others holding their coats, all of them trying to keep from being attacked by the savage, red-headed, wild-eyed . . . squirrel.

This wasn't your typical furry, nut-loving little creature. This crazed critter had already attacked one woman and was harassing others. The hostages breathed a sigh of relief when they saw Officer Oskierko outside their office. "They kept saying 'Get it out of here. Get it out of here,'" Oskierko said.

Oskierko slowly entered the premises, and when the squirrel's back was turned, he made a lunge at him—and the hostages heard a loud tear. Oskierko's pants had split during the assault; he radioed for reinforcements (for both himself and his pants). Other officers arrived and soon they had the cagey culprit captive.

The police turned the furry felon over to a veterinarian, who planned to examine the squirrel for rabies. Iron bars do not a prison make, and for this little woodland creature a plastic cage didn't make a very good prison either. He nibbled and gnawed his way through the cage, attacked the vet and others, and escaped. The squirrel is still on the lam.

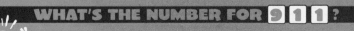

HOLD THE ANCHOVIES

DISPATCHER: "911. What is your emergency?"

MALE CALLER: "Yeah, I want to order a pizza."

DISPATCHER: "You need to call 411."

A ROSE BY ANY OTHER NAME

911: "911. Please state the nature of your emergency."

CALLER: "I just thought you'd like to know that someone has trespassed on my property."

911: "Okay, ma'am. Was anything damaged or taken?"

CALLER: "That's why I called. Someone had trimmed my rose bushes. Now, I'm the only one who trims my bushes, and I would know when they'd been trimmed. I just thought you'd like to know. I think my next-door neighbor did it. She's a mean old bitch."

A FISHY STORY

We've all heard about the goldfish-swallowing craze that happened during the 1950s—but one Akron, Ohio, man took this nostalgic notion and gave it a fatal twist. Twenty-three-year-old Michael Gentner, on a dare, attempted to swallow a live fish in January 1998. Not a big deal, one might think, but this was a big fish—a five-inch-long fish to be exact. The fish lodged in Gentner's throat, and he could neither swallow it nor spit it out. His friends called 911 but told the operator only that their friend had eaten some fish.

When the paramedics arrived, they thought they were about to deal with a routine food-choking incident and were completely surprised when they saw the tail of the still live fish flapping in Gentner's mouth. Gentner, however, was no longer breathing. Paramedics extracted the fish, but they were unable to resuscitate Genter, and he was later pronounced dead.

Deputy Police Chief Michael Matulavich said Gentner had apparently swallowed fish on a dare before. "It's a stunt," Matulavich said. "People swallow live fish, but not one this large. That may have been the lure of the dare." Gentner's three friends aren't likely to be charged, Matulavich said. "I don't know what you'd charge them on. If I dare you to jump off a bridge and you do it, and you're twenty-three years of age, you're stupid," Matulavich said. "I don't know what would prompt somebody to do something like that." In case you're wondering, the fish didn't survive the ordeal either.

911 REPORT:

"My neighbor's dog is barking."

911? HIGH, HOW ARE YOU?

The Sioux Falls, South Dakota, 911 center received a 911 hang-up call which originated from the apartment of Shari Sue Kjellsen. A patrol car was dispatched to make sure the woman was all right. When police arrived they found the only problem with the woman was that she was a little too honest. She told the officers she originally called 911 to complain because a male acquaintance had taken her marijuana. But, she assured them, everything was okay now because he brought it back. Police informed her that things weren't okay and proceeded to seize her pot, arrest her, and take her to court. She pleaded guilty to drug possession and was fined $100. Lt. Mark Moberly reported that Kjellsen didn't appear stoned when she called 911. "Some people are just kind of naturally high," he said. "Especially out here where the air is so clear."

REPORT . . . 911 REPORT . . . 911 REPO
. 911 REPORT . . . 911 REPORT . . . 911
REPORT . . . 911 REPORT . . . 911 REPO
. 911 REPORT . . . 911 REPORT . . . 911
REPORT . . . 911 REPORT . . . 911 REPO
. 911 REPORT . . . 911 REPORT . . . 911
REPORT . . . 911 REPORT . . . 911 REPO
. 911 REPORT . . . 911 REPORT . . . 911

"What's the phone number
for police?"

REPORT . . . 911 REPORT . . . 911 REPO
. 911 REPORT . . . 911 REPORT . . . 911
REPORT . . . 911 REPORT . . . 911 REPO
. 911 REPORT . . . 911 REPORT . . . 911
REPORT . . . 911 REPORT . . . 911 REPO
. 911 REPORT . . . 911 REPORT . . . 911
REPORT . . . 911 REPORT . . . 911 REPO

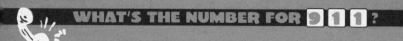

A PAIN IN THE NECK

DISPATCHER: "Ambulance emergency line."

MAN: "Hello?"

DISPATCHER: "Yes."

MAN: "Who is this?"

DISPATCHER: "This is the ambulance emergency line. Do you have an emergency?"

MAN: "I need an ambulance."

DISPATCHER: "Who is this?"

MAN: "Uh, Joe."

DISPATCHER: "Okay, Joe. Where do you need us?"

MAN: "I'm the in the m—f— phone booth."

DISPATCHER: "Okay, what's the address there?"

MAN: "Hold on."

DISPATCHER: "Okay, sir, did you call through 911?"

MAN: "No."

DISPATCHER: "Okay, Joe, I need a location. What street are you on?"

MAN: "Uh, I'm in the m—f— phone booth at
the Stop & Go. Yeah, that's it. I'm at the
m—f— Stop & Go. On, uh, wait a minute.
On, uh, Howsmith . . . what's the m—f—
street? Howsmith and Corville and
Howsmith. At the m—f— Stop & Go."

DISPATCHER: "Howsmith, Corville and what?"

MAN: "Hold on."

*(The Dispatcher continues typing the information.
There is a pause.)*

MAN: "It's Joe!"

DISPATCHER: "Uh, huh."

MAN: "How 'bout it. Let me see, Coffee, Comfee?"

DISPATCHER: "Comfey?"

MAN: "There you go. There you go. I'm in the
m—f— phone booth. Let me tell you
what. I'm at the . . . I'm going down the
m—f— road driving in my car minding
my own g—d— business, and a m—f—
deer jumps out and hits my car."

DISPATCHER: "Okay, sir. Are you injured?"

MAN: "Let . . . now, let me tell you. I get out and pick the m—f— deer up. I thought he dead. I put the m—f— deer in my backseat, and I'm driving down the m—f— road and minding my own business. The m—f— woke up and bit me in the back of my g—d— neck, and he bit me and he done kicked the sh-t out of my car. I'm in the m—f— phone booth. The deer bit me in the neck. A big m—f— dog came up and bit me in the leg, and I hit him with the m—f— tire iron, and I stabbed him. I stabbed him with my knife. So, I got a hurt leg, and the m—f— deer bit me in the neck. And the deer . . . the dog won't let me out of the m—f— phone booth, 'cause he wants the deer. Now, who gets the deer, me or the dog?"

DISPATCHER: "Okay, sir. Are you injured?"

MAN: "Yeah, m—f— deer bit me in the neck. Hold on. Let . . . hey, the m—f— dog is biting me! Hold on! The m—f— dog is biting me. Hold on! G—d— it, get out of here. Hold on! The m—f— dog is biting my ass. Hold on!"

(The caller hangs up the phone.)

WELL, BITE ME TOO!

A midnight 911 call came in from a mother of a three-year-old child. The woman told the dispatcher that her child was having a severe allergic reaction to an insect bite. A team of paramedics were on their way in a matter of minutes. When they arrived they found the child sitting on her mother's lap. The child appeared to be breathing normally and showed no outward signs of an allergic reaction—no swelling, no rash. The paramedics questioned the mother, and the woman told them her child had been bitten by a mosquito. When they examined the little girl, the paramedics were at a loss to find the bite—all they found were light scratch marks that hadn't even scraped the skin. It was then that the mother explained that the mosquito had bitten her daughter about four days ago. Waiting that long was a stupid mistake—now they'll never be able to track down the mosquito for questioning.

911 REPORT:

Male complainant called because he didn't want to bother looking up Sheriff's Office phone number in phone book.

DÉJÀ VU AGAIN

Larry Edwards, a convenience store clerk in Asheville, North Carolina, who had just been robbed, was on the phone to a 911 dispatcher in November 1992 giving the details of the robbery. Suddenly, according to the 911 operator, Edwards screamed and dropped the phone. He was being robbed again. The second robber became irate when he discovered that Edwards' cash register was empty. The thief thought the clerk was lying when he explained that he had just been robbed. Out of frustration, the crook slashed Edwards' arm on the way out of the store.

REPORT . . . 911 REPORT . . . 911 REP
. 911 REPORT . . . 911 REPORT . . . 911
REPORT . . . 911 REPORT . . . 911 REP
. 911 REPORT . . . 911 REPORT . . . 911
REPORT . . . 911 REPORT . . . 911 REP
. 911 REPORT . . . 911 REPORT . . . 911
REPORT . . . 911 REPORT . . . 911 REP
. 911 REPORT . . . 911 REPORT . . . 911

"Why is 1244 [another police phone number] busy?"

. 911 REPORT . . . 911 REPORT . . . 911
REPORT . . . 911 REPORT . . . 911 REP
. 911 REPORT . . . 911 REPORT . . . 911
REPORT . . . 911 REPORT . . . 911 REP
. 911 REPORT . . . 911 REPORT . . . 911
REPORT . . . 911 REPORT . . . 911 REP
. 911 REPORT . . . 911 REPORT . . . 911

REPORT . . . 911 REPORT . . . 911 REP

A GRAINY IMAGE

Several calls came into the 911 center when a huge grain elevator exploded. Here is the transcript of one of the more interesting calls.

911:   "911."

CALLER SIX: "Yes, I need to report an emergency."

911:   "Is this at Garvey Grain? Where at, sir?"

CALLER: "I live at, uh, the . . . on Fourth Street."

911:   "OK, what happened?"

CALLER: "It felt like something ran into my house. I come outside, and there's a great big cloud of smoke just southwest."

911:   "OK, we just got a report that Garvey Grain just blew up. Would that be it?"

CALLER: "That's probably what it is."

911:   "OK, sir, is everything OK at your house?"

CALLER: "Yes."

911:   "All right, then. Bye."

CALLER: "Bye."

THE CAT'S MEOW

Dispatcher Elena Arroyo thought she'd heard it all until she received a call from a cat. The Tampa, Florida, 911 operator heard a choking, meowing sound and shouted to her supervisor "Oh, my God—it's a cat on the phone." Deputy Joe Bamford arrived at the residence and discovered that the cat was choking on its own collar. Tipper, a gray-and-white, nine-month-old cat had knocked the phone off the hook and pushed "1" on the preprogrammed keypad, which dialed the emergency number. Owner Gail Curtis was glad the cat was saved but stated, "I just hope he doesn't start dialing long-distance."

The next summer Tipper suffered through another ordeal—a possible cat-napping. The cat had pawed his way to fame with this 911 call and in October 1996 suddenly disappeared from Curtis's home. She had tethered the cat outdoors, and when she came back to get him, he was gone. Three days later, however, the cat reappeared at his home in the Flying Cloud Mobile Home Park unscathed, and was reunited with his owners. No call for alarm!

911 REPORT ... 911 REPORT ... 911 REPORT
911 REPORT ... 911 REPORT ... 911
911 REPORT ... 911 REPORT ...
911 REPORT ... 911 REPORT ... 911
911 REPORT ... 911 REPORT ... 911 REPORT
911 REPORT ... 911 REPORT ... 911
911 REPORT ... 911 REPORT ... 911 REPORT

"What were the winning
numbers for the Evening
Pick Four today?"

911 REPORT ... 911 REPORT ... 911 REPORT
911 REPORT ... 911 REPORT ... 911
911 REPORT ... 911 REPORT ... 911 REPORT
911 REPORT ... 911 REPORT ... 911
911 REPORT ... 911 REPORT ... 911 REPORT
911 REPORT ... 911 REPORT ... 911

911 REPORT ... 911 REPORT ... 911 REPORT

IF THE TRUTH BE KNOWN

911: "911. Fire or emergency?"

CALLER: "Neither. My son was bothering me. I just wanted to let you know."

ROOM WITH A VIEW

911: "911. What's the nature of your emergency?"

WOMAN *(whispering)*: "Is this 911?"

911: "Yes, ma'am. It is."

WOMAN *(whispering)*: "Oh, good. I'm glad I finally got someone who can help me."

911: "Are you in trouble, ma'am?"

WOMAN *(whispering)*: "Oh, yes, yes. A lot of trouble, I believe."

911: "Is someone in the room with you?"

WOMAN *(whispering)*: "No. I don't see anyone."

911: "Then why are you whispering? What's your emergency?"

WOMAN: "I'm a hospital patient, and I think an orderly wants to see me naked."

SOMEONE'S BEEN
SLEEPING IN MY BED

According to a call received by a Madison, Wisconsin, police officer, a man dialed 911 to complain of an intruder. The twenty-six-year-old man explained to the officer that he had gotten up in the middle of the night to go to the bathroom and when he returned a stranger, wearing only boxer shorts, was sleeping in his bed. Skeptical of the call but following regulations, the 911 operator dispatched an officer to the residence. The officer on the scene discovered the man wasn't lying—there was someone sleeping in his bed, and it wasn't Goldilocks. The slumbering stranger turned out to be a very intoxicated twenty-two-year-old college student from DePere, Wisconsin. Hmm . . . an intoxicated college student—never heard of one of those before.

911 REPORT:

"Complainant says unknown male has been living in her house. Complainant is partially blind and just found his clothing."

BREAK LIKE THE WIND

In December 1997, police in Janesville, Wisconsin, responded to a 911 dispatcher to check out a domestic disturbance call. When police arrived at the location, they were told the situation by the wife. She claimed the argument started when she and her husband were tucking their son into bed—and the husband inappropriately passed gas.

911 REPORT . . . 911 REPORT . . . 911 REP
911 REPORT . . . 911 REPORT . . . 911
911 REPORT . . . 911 REPORT . . . 911 REP
911 REPORT . . . 911 REPORT . . . 911
911 REPORT . . . 911 REPORT . . . 911 REP
911 REPORT . . . 911 REPORT . . . 911
911 REPORT . . . 911 REPORT . . . 911 REP
911 REPORT . . . 911 REPORT . . . 911

"Just wanted to check and see
if it was really working."

911 REPORT . . . 911 REPORT . . . 911 REP
911 REPORT . . . 911 REPORT . . . 911
911 REPORT . . . 911 REPORT . . . 911 REP
911 REPORT . . . 911 REPORT . . . 911
911 REPORT . . . 911 REPORT . . . 911 REP
911 REPORT . . . 911 REPORT . . . 911

911 REPORT . . . 911 REPORT . . . 911 REP

BOSOM BUDDIES, LIFELONG PALS

911: "911. Fire or emergency."

CALLER: "Um, *(cough)* emergency, I guess."

911: "What's the nature of your emergency, sir?"

CALLER: "*(Cough.)* You see, my friend, Jack, we've been drinking, you see, and suddenly he just falls over on the floor there."

911: "How much have you had to drink?"

CALLER: "Not enough for that to happen, man. *(Cough.)* We've been more drunk than this before—lots of times. This is a first. He don't look so good. You probably ought to send someone around real soon."

911: "Is he breathing?"

CALLER: "I'll check." *(He puts phone down. Pause. He gets back on the line.)* "I don't think so— not like he normally breathes, you know. He don't look too good."

911: "Do you want to do CPR till the paramedics arrive?"

CALLER: "I can't do that. I still have a bad cold."

TROPHY BRIDE

911: "911. What's your emergency?"

CALLER: "It's my old lady. She's gone crazy!"

911: "What's the problem, sir?"

CALLER: "She's tearing through the house, throwing sh-t around. Broke out a g—d— window with my f—g bowling trophy. She said she's going to kill me, man. F—g hell, I believe her too!"

911: "Does she have any weapons?"

CALLER: "Well, she has real long fingernails."

NEARLY HOG HEAVEN

Tracy Mosier, 911 dispatcher from Kelso, Washington, was trained in giving instructions on the Heimlich maneuver. So she was ready when this call came in. Well, maybe she was ready. "My pig! She's choked and she's passed out." Mosier calmly coached the woman on the other end of the line step by step until the pig was revived. Mosier was happy to help—she also is proficient, she says, in giving mouth-to-snout resuscitation.

911 REPORT

"Can you tell me when the next earthquake is?"

DON'T CRY OVER
SPILLED BEER

The phone rang at the 911 dispatch center in Des Moines, Iowa—but it was a hang-up. Following procedure, a police officer was dispatched to the residence on the screen to see if there was any trouble. When they arrived, police discovered the reason for the phone call was an error. Forty-nine-year-old Jerry Bentley had inadvertently dialed 911 while wiping up spilled beer from his phone. Police ran a routine check and discovered that Bentley had an outstanding warrant for his arrest on drug possession and failure to appear in court. Bentley's day went from "It's Miller Time" to "It's Prison Time."

911 REPORT ... 911 REPORT ... 911 REPO
911 REPORT ... 911 REPORT ... 911
RT ... **911 REPORT ... 911 REPORT .**
911 REPORT ... 911 REPORT ... 911
911 REPORT ... 911 REPORT ... 911 REPO
911 REPORT ... 911 REPORT ... 911
911 REPORT ... 911 REPORT ... 911 REPO
911 REPORT ... 911 REPORT ... 911

"These bee droppings
are ruining my roof!"

911 REPORT ... 911 REPORT ... 911 REPO
911 REPORT ... 911 REPORT ... 911
911 REPORT ... 911 REPORT ... 911 REPO
911 REPORT ... 911 REPORT ... 911
911 REPORT ... 911 REPORT ... 911 REPO
911 REPORT ... 911 REPORT ... 911

911 REPORT ... 911 REPORT ... 911 REPO

DEEP THROAT RETURNS

911: "911. Fire or emergency."

MAN: "I know what you're up to."

911: "Excuse me, sir?"

MAN: "I can't excuse you. I know what you've been doing and who you are and don't think I don't know."

911: "I'm sorry, sir. Do you have an emergency to report?"

MAN: "I'm going to report each of you to the CIA— you'll go to jail for what you've been doing."

911: "I'm sorry, sir. I don't understand what you're talking about."

MAN: "Sure you don't. I've got the number of the Secret Service, and they're already on to you guys. Don't say I didn't warn you!"

(Caller hangs up.)

ONE WORD—SOUNDS LIKE . . .

911 DISPATCHER: "911. What's your emergency?"

CALLER: "Uh, my grandfather just died. Can you send someone around here to pick him up."

911 DISPATCHER: "You say your grandfather died?"

CALLER: "Yeah, a few minutes ago, I guess. He was real old, and he's been sick awhile. He finally just died."

911 DISPATCHER: "Could you give me your address, please?"

CALLER: "Sure. It's the Fall Vista Apartments on Thurgood. Apartment 34 D."

911 DISPATCHER: "Apartment 34 . . . "

CALLER: *"D, D, as in dead."*

A CRACK IN THE CASE

A local 911 operator in Houston, Texas, received a call from Linda Marie Davis, who complained about an unconscionable consumer fraud that a local merchant had perpetrated. Davis said she had just bought some inferior-quality crack cocaine and thought the proper authorities should know about the rip-off. The stunned 911 operator told Davis to wait by the pay phone from which she was calling until an officer arrived to take her statement. Davis did just that. When the police arrived, Davis was still angry. She showed the police the rock of cocaine and was surprised when, instead of expressing their sympathy, they arrested her. Davis was right, however; lab results showed the crack to be only 30 percent pure—but Davis was 100 percent stupid.

911 REPORT:

''When is my power coming back on?''

I CAN'T BEAR IT!

FIRST CALL

911 OPERATOR: "May I help you?"

YOUNG WOMAN: "Um, yes. I'm calling because I just saw a black bear . . ." *(Giggling is heard in the background)* "Stop laughing. Um, a black bear ran across the road right by our houses."

911 OPERATOR (in a flat, skeptical voice): "A bear?"

YOUNG WOMAN: "Yes. Uh, yeah. Right by Oceana."

VOICE IN BACKGROUND: "Stop laughing. Stop it. It's possible."

911 OPERATOR: "You're sure it was a bear?"

YOUNG WOMAN: "I'm positive. I, I stopped my car and I checked twice. It turned around and looked at me. It was a bear."

911 OPERATOR: "I'll get someone out to talk to you."

SECOND CALL

MAN: "OK. This is going to sound really weird, but I just saw a black bear."

911 OPERATOR: "OK, where are you at now?"

MAN: "I'm in my house now."

911 OPERATOR: "Was it in the woods, or where was it?"

MAN: "It was on Southern Boulevard, right down the street from my house, crossing the railroad tracks. Toward Virginia Beach Boulevard."

911 OPERATOR: "OK, were you in a vehicle or what?"

MAN: "I was driving by."

911 OPERATOR: "How long ago was this, sir?"

MAN: "About ten minutes."

911 OPERATOR: "All right, I'll get an officer to go down and check."

Just in case you're wondering, game officials shot the two-year-old bear with a tranquilizer, tagged it, and released it in the Great Dismal Swamp Wildlife Refuge in Virginia.

THE ROAD LESS TRAVELED

Since becoming mayor of Scottsdale, Arizona, in April 1997, Sam Campana has called 911 on six different occasions. Is Scottsdale so riddled with crime that the mayor had to make so many calls? Or was Campana ill or did she need police assistance? Nope. She was lost. Each of the six calls Campana made to 911 was to ask for directions to official functions while she was in her car. Not wanting to bust the mayor for making frivolous 911 calls, the police, after the sixth and last call, sent Campana a memo informing her that 911 is for emergency use only—they also supplied her with three police telephone numbers. Seems to me they should have given her a map. And women say men are bad with directions.

911 REPORT ... 911 REPORT ... 911 REPORT ... 911 REPORT ... 911
911 REPORT ... 911 REPORT ... 911
REPORT ... 911 REPORT ... 911 REPORT ... 911 REPORT ... 911
REPORT ... 911 REPORT ... 911 REPORT ... 911 REPORT ... 911
REPORT ... 911 REPORT ... 911 REPORT

"There's a rat in my house.
Could you please send
someone over to kill it?"

REPORT ... 911 REPORT ... 911 REPORT
911 REPORT ... 911 REPORT ... 911
REPORT ... 911 REPORT ... 911 REPORT
911 REPORT ... 911 REPORT ... 911
REPORT ... 911 REPORT ... 911 REPORT
911 REPORT ... 911 REPORT ... 911

NUTS FOR KNOTS

Police in Houma, Louisiana, issued a citation in April 1992 to Velma Ann Wantlin for improper use of the 911 emergency line. Wantlin, twenty-eight at the time, called 911 to report the following emergency situation: her husband was preventing her from watching the season finale of *Knots Landing*.

911 REPORT:

"Would you send the Fire Department to our address? We need them to get our pet parakeet out of a tree."

MUST BE THE NEW MATH

911: "911, what's the nature of your emergency, please?"

WOMAN: "I'm trying to reach nine-eleven, but my phone doesn't have an eleven on it."

911: "This is nine-eleven."

WOMAN: "I thought you just said it was nine-one-one."

911: "Yes, ma'am. Nine-one-one and nine-eleven are the same thing."

WOMAN: "Honey, I may be old, but I'm not stupid!"

IF THE CAR'S A-ROCKIN' . . .

In Vancouver two city police cars, responding to a 911 emergency call about a stolen vehicle accidentally crashed head-on. Fortunately the officers weren't badly hurt. It turned out that the emergency wasn't a stolen sedan but a cuddling codger. This unusual event started when a man called 911 to report his father's car was being stolen. After police got out of their wrecked cruisers, they were shocked when they didn't discover any thieves—just the seventy-two-year-old owner of the car and a female prostitute. It turns out that the son was upset with his father for routinely hiring prostitutes and called 911 hoping it would deter his father's activity. And they say an old dog can't turn new tricks.

911 REPORT . . . 911 REPORT . . . 911 REP
. 911 REPORT . . . 911 REPORT . . . 911
REPORT . . . 911 REPORT . . . 911 REP
. 911 REPORT . . . 911 REPORT . . . 911
REPORT . . . 911 REPORT . . . 911 REP
. 911 REPORT . . . 911 REPORT . . . 911
REPORT . . . 911 REPORT . . . 911 REP

"Uh, I need some help.
Seems I locked my keys
in the car again."

REPORT . . . 911 REPORT . . . 911 REP
. 911 REPORT . . . 911 REPORT . . . 911
REPORT . . . 911 REPORT . . . 911 REP
. 911 REPORT . . . 911 REPORT . . . 911
REPORT . . . 911 REPORT . . . 911 REP
. 911 REPORT . . . 911 REPORT . . . 911
REPORT . . . 911 REPORT . . . 911 REP

DRIVEN TO EXTREMES

DISPATCHER: "911. Fire or emergency?"

CALLER: "This is Ed Farnham at 247 Oak Terrace Drive. I put an ad in the paper selling my 1992 Dodge Dart, and some guy wanted a test drive. That was three hours ago, and he hasn't come back."

911: "We'll need a description of him."

CALLER: "He's a lawyer."

UNCLEAR RECEPTION

911: "911. What's your emergency?"

CALLER: "I want to report a consumer fraud, please."

911: "Ma'am, 911 is for emergencies only."

CALLER: "Well, I don't know who else to call.
My television set doesn't work. The man
I bought it from won't give me my money
back."

I'LL GIVE YOUR HIDE
A GOOD TANNING

When a 911 dispatcher alerted police and firefighters to a residence where the female occupant was stuck in a tanning bed, they thought it might be their lucky day. But when they arrived at the Norton Shores, Michigan, home of Cecilia Wolcott, what they found was a sixty-year-old naked woman who "got quite a tan." Wolcott had purchased the tanning bed to treat a skin condition, but the first time she tried it out, she accidentally slipped and the lid got stuck. She couldn't get the lid up and couldn't turn the tanning machine off. The bed "was lit up and it was getting plenty warm," Wolcott said. "I knew I'd burn to a crisp if I didn't get some help." Luckily for her (but a little strange, if you ask me), Wolcott had taken her cordless phone into the tanning bed with her, and she used it to call 911. Police and firefighters immediately pulled the plug on the machine and then worked to get Wolcott out. While the scorched senior citizen stood before police and firefighters, they couldn't tell if she was red from embarrassment or just well done.

911 REPORT . . . 911 REPORT . . . 911 REP
911 REPORT . . . 911 REPORT . . . 911
REPORT . . . 911 REPORT . . . 911 REP
911 REPORT . . . 911 REPORT . . . 911
REPORT . . . 911 REPORT . . . 911 REP
911 REPORT . . . 911 REPORT . . . 911
REPORT . . . 911 REPORT . . . 911 REP
911 REPORT . . . 911 REPORT . . . 911

"Is it all right in Boulder
to ask a woman for sex?"

REPORT . . . 911 REPORT . . . 911 REP
911 REPORT . . . 911 REPORT . . . 911
REPORT . . . 911 REPORT . . . 911 REP
911 REPORT . . . 911 REPORT . . . 911
REPORT . . . 911 REPORT . . . 911 REP
911 REPORT . . . 911 REPORT . . . 911
REPORT . . . 911 REPORT . . . 911 REP

TAKE A DEEP BREATH

911 DISPATCHER: "911. Fire or emergency?"

CALLER: "Emergency. I need you to . . . I need an ambulance. Quick! Send one now!"

911 DISPATCHER: "What's the emergency, sir?"

CALLER: "It's my Uncle. He's unconscious and I can't get him to wake up. Get an ambulance down here now. The address is 68 North Hampton. Hurry up!"

911 DISPATCHER: "Settle down, sir, and try to remain calm. An ambulance is on the way. Is your uncle breathing?"

CALLER: "He's not breathing!"

911 DISPATCHER: "Can you get the phone close to him?"

CALLER: "*Why?* You want to hear he's not breathing, too?"

HIS BARK IS WORSE THAN HIS BITE

It was a Norman Rockwell Christmas. The stockings were hung by the chimney with care, the tree was decorated, and the dog was about to vomit on the carpet. When ten-year-old John Roemer saw his nauseated dog, Pookie, about to puck he rushed over and pushed the dog off the rug. Suddenly, the family's large artificial tree fell over nearly crushing the little boy. So keeping one eye on the cramping canine John pushed the tree back into its stand and then moved back to look at his handiwork. That's when the tree fell again—this time pinning little John under it. He couldn't get up, he couldn't get the tree off, and the dog's cheeks were starting to puff out again. John was able to reach a cordless phone, and he called several neighbors to help him out from under the Christmas tree. Most weren't home in his Fremont, Nebraska, neighborhood and one "didn't believe me," said John. He finally dialed 911 and explained his situation. But 911 dispatchers have heard it all before, and they believed the boy was pinned by the pine. Police and firefighters freed the young boy who wasn't hurt by the "Bonzi" tree.

911 REPORT . . . 911 REPORT . . . 911 REP
. 911 REPORT . . . 911 REPORT . . . 911
RT . . . 911 REPORT . . . 911 REPORT .
. 911 REPORT . . . 911 REPORT . . . 911
911 REPORT . . . 911 REPORT . . . 911 REP
. 911 REPORT . . . 911 REPORT . . . 911
911 REPORT . . . 911 REPORT . . . 911 REP

"Where the hell are
my food stamps?
I'm a taxpayer, you know!"

911 REPORT . . . 911 REPORT . . . 911 REP
. 911 REPORT . . . 911 REPORT . . . 911
911 REPORT . . . 911 REPORT . . . 911 REP
. 911 REPORT . . . 911 REPORT . . . 911
911 REPORT . . . 911 REPORT . . . 911 REP
. 911 REPORT . . . 911 REPORT . . . 911

911 REPORT . . . 911 REPORT . . . 911 REP

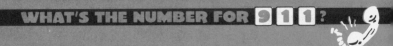

THE BLAME GAME

DISPATCHER: "Akron 911. What is your emergency?"

MAN: "My old lady's going nuts. I don't want the blame for it. She's drunk. She bolted out the door. No shoes. No coat. I don't want the blame."

EAR-ITATING NEIGHBOR

911 DISPATCHER: "Akron 911. What's your emergency?"

CALLER: "There's this woman, you know? She lives in my neighborhood. She sticks something sharp in my ear. Will you tell her to stop it?"

AND THE NUMBER IS . . .

What's the emergency number? 911, right? Yes, but not if you live in Australia. The number there is "000." Unfortunately, when a Sydney, Australia, businessman saw a fire in his building, he dialed 911 instead. The man, whose name wasn't released, had just finished watching the U.S. television series "Rescue 911" when he noticed the blaze. The nine minutes he wasted by mistakenly dialing 911 caused more than $188,000 in damages, according to an Australian firefighter spokesman. A shop owner on the ground floor who also saw the fire called the correct number. And they say people aren't influenced by what they see on television.

911 REPORT:

Thirteen-year-old stubbed her toe on a stereo speaker.

UP IN SMOKE

"I made some stupid mistakes," admitted a thirty-year-old Maryland man to the judge at his sentencing. Several months before, the man had called 911 to report a fire on his property. "You gotta put out the fire, man," he told the dispatcher. "My marijuana plants are burning." When the fire-fighting team arrived, they discovered the man sitting in the kitchen with the lights out playing his guitar. He was arrested. Apparently, he was arrested both legally and mentally.

REPORT ... 911 REPORT ... 911 REP
911 REPORT ... 911 REPORT ... 911
REPORT ... 911 REPORT ... 911 REP
911 REPORT ... 911 REPORT ... 911
REPORT ... 911 REPORT ... 911 REP
911 REPORT ... 911 REPORT ... 911
REPORT ... 911 REPORT ... 911 REP

Person answered "no"
to the question,
"Are you conscious?"

REPORT ... 911 REPORT ... 911 REP
911 REPORT ... 911 REPORT ... 911
REPORT ... 911 REPORT ... 911 REP
911 REPORT ... 911 REPORT ... 911
REPORT ... 911 REPORT ... 911 REP
911 REPORT ... 911 REPORT ... 911
REPORT ... 911 REPORT ... 911 REP

IS IT REAL OR IS IT MEMOREX?

DISPATCHER: "911. Please state your emergency."

MALE CALLER: "Yeah, am I talking to a real operator or is this a recording?"

DISPATCHER: "This is a real operator. Please state your emergency."

MALE CALLER: "Are you sure you're a real person? You sort of sound like a recording."

DISPATCHER *(irritated)*: "I'm a real person, sir!"

MALE CALLER: "Okay. Now you sound like a real operator."

I'M NOT THE MAN I USED TO BE

DISPATCHER: "911. What's your emergency?"

CALLER: "Could you send the police to my house?"

DISPATCHER: "What's wrong there?"

CALLER: "I called and someone answered the phone, but I'm not there."

YOU'RE ONLY AS OLD AS YOU FEEL

A ninety-year-old man called the Charlotte, North Carolina, emergency center to complain of a consumer fraud. He told the shocked dispatcher that he had recently hired a prostitute and she had left him, well, dissatisfied. He wanted to file a formal complaint, have the prostitute arrested, and get his money returned. The dispatcher explained to the man that solicitation of prostitution was a crime. He quickly hung up the phone. Makes you wonder if, at his age, he was offered a senior citizen's discount.

REPORT . . . 911 REPORT . . . 911 REP
911 REPORT . . . 911 REPORT . . . 911
REPORT . . . 911 REPORT . . . 911 REP
911 REPORT . . . 911 REPORT . . . 911
REPORT . . . 911 REPORT . . . 911 REP
911 REPORT . . . 911 REPORT . . . 911
REPORT . . . 911 REPORT . . . 911 REP
911 REPORT . . . 911 REPORT . . . 911

"I've been standing all day, and my feet hurt."

REPORT . . . 911 REPORT . . . 911 REP
911 REPORT . . . 911 REPORT . . . 911
REPORT . . . 911 REPORT . . . 911 REP
911 REPORT . . . 911 REPORT . . . 911
REPORT . . . 911 REPORT . . . 911 REP
911 REPORT . . . 911 REPORT . . . 911
REPORT . . . 911 REPORT . . . 911 REP

BEER NUTS

In June 1996 a man in La Vergne, Tennessee, called the emergency 911 number and requested they send a squad car to his residence. The man explained that he and his wife had had a fight and he needed police to come to his house and stop his wife from pouring out all his beer.

911 REPORT

Dispatcher to police: "Meet complainant regarding a neighbor's rabbit eating complainant's garden."

THE 411 ON 911

**PALM BEACH
911 DISPATCHER:** "911 emergency."

CALLER: "Hi, I've been getting a lot of calls for someone else, and, uh, I need to, you . . . I would like a different number and uh . . . "

**PALM BEACH
911 DISPATCHER:** "Are you calling 911 because you need your phone number changed?"

CALLER: "Yes."

**PALM BEACH
911 DISPATCHER:** "Have you called the phone company?"

CALLER: "I'm not sure how to get in touch with them—but I knew 911."

**PALM BEACH
911 DISPATCHER:** "Look at your phone bill. That's the number you would need to call to get your phone number changed."

CALLER: "Oh, could you connect me?"

FRICTION BURNS

911 DISPATCHER: "911. Fire or emergency?"

YOUNG BOY: "Yeah, there's a fire here. Help, help. Send someone."

911 DISPATCHER: "Just settle down, son. What's your name?"

(The caller hangs up. The Charlotte, North Carolina, 911 dispatcher locates the address and phone number from the Enhanced 911 computer display and calls back the residence. A woman answers the phone.)

911 DISPATCHER: "This is the emergency 911 operator. We received a call that there was a fire at this residence."

WOMAN (*confused*): "No . . . I don't understand. There's nothing wrong here. . . . I don't know why. . . . Uh, no, no, sorry, no fire here."

911 DISPATCHER: "We recently received a phone call from a young boy at this number reporting a fire. We were just double-checking."

WOMAN: "No, there's no fire here. But as soon as I hang up, there's going to be a fire on my son's backside."

HO, HO, WHAT!

On Christmas morning, 1996, Scott Kane and his wife heard someone prowling around in their home in Chevy Chase, Maryland, and called 911. Despite the blaring sirens and screeching tires of several squad cars, and then the noise of seven police officers storming into the living room, twenty-three-year-old Roger Augusto Sosa, who had broken into the couple's home, was still sitting happily under the Christmas tree opening the Kanes' presents.

911 REPORT:

Caller: "I'd like to make a unanimous complaint, so don't use my name."

A TONGUE-AND-CHEEK SITUATION

Two-year-old Melissa Garman was doing what any other two-year-old child does—making a racket. On this particular day in August 1991, she was in the care of her fourteen-year-old uncle, Duane Della. Pretty soon, however, the constant noise got the best of Duane.

"I was in the freezer looking for something to eat, and I bent over to yell at her," said Della. But when he bent over his tongue got stuck to the freezer. Duane, as best he could, told Melissa to drag her high chair over to the telephone, pick it up, and bring it to him. She did. Duane punched out the number 911 and a dispatcher quickly answered.

"We couldn't understand what he was saying," recalled one officer. Duane finally made himself understood, and soon rescuers were at his front door. A cup of warm water on Duane's tongue did the trick, and he was free. He thanked his niece for helping him out of a frosty situation, and he promised to mind his tongue from then on.

REPORT ... 911 REPORT ... 911 REP
. 911 REPORT ... 911 REPORT ... 911
RT ... 911 REPORT ... 911 REPORT .
. 911 REPORT ... 911 REPORT ... 911
REPORT ... 911 REPORT ... 911 REP
. 911 REPORT ... 911 REPORT ... 911
REPORT ... 911 REPORT ... 911 REP

Male complainant called to
inform that there is a squirrel
on his front porch.

REPORT ... 911 REPORT ... 911 REP
. 911 REPORT ... 911 REPORT ... 911
REPORT ... 911 REPORT ... 911 REP
. 911 REPORT ... 911 REPORT ... 911
REPORT ... 911 REPORT ... 911 REP
. 911 REPORT ... 911 REPORT ... 911

REPORT ... 911 REPORT ... 911 REP

A GREAT FIRST DATE

911: "911. What's your emergency?"

MAN: "I'm at this woman's house, and we're about to have a couple of drinks, and suddenly she just drops . . . just like that, she drops on the floor."

911: "All right, sir, just relax."

MAN: "She's just laying there. I didn't do nothing, I swear!"

911: "No one said that you did, sir. Can you tell if she's breathing?"

MAN: "Gee, I don't know."

911: "What's the address?"

MAN: "The Brookside apartments on Western. She lives at, uh, apartment, oh sh-t, uh, apartment 14D, that's it."

911: "Sir, I'm going to tell you how to do CPR, so that you can help her."

MAN: "No, I don't think so. I haven't known her that long."

A ZIT ON ZAT

DISPATCHER: "Emergency. Ambulance."

CALLER: "Yeah, I wanted to know if you can help me. I have a pimple on my penis and it popped and there is puss coming out of it. I don't know what to do."

DISPATCHER: "OK, I will send someone over to help you . . . I think."

I NEED THAT LIKE
I NEED A HOLE IN THE HEAD

Eighteen-year-old Joseph Trevor Kale picked up his phone to call a friend and received a shooting pain when the phone exploded and electrocuted him. At least that's what he thought had happened. Kale called 911 and asked for help. When emergency personnel arrived at his home, they concluded things had happened a little differently. Yes, the phone had exploded, but that was because Kale had been shot in the head and the bullet had passed through the phone first. The man was listed in critical but stable condition—the shooter and the motive for the shooting were never discovered.

911 REPORT:

"I can't sleep."

THE WRITING IS ON THE WALL

911: "911. Please state your emergency."

CALLER: "I'm scared."

911: "What's the problem, miss?"

CALLER: "I just got a Ouija board for my birthday, and now there's writing on my wall and I can't get it off. . . . This thing is going back to Kmart first thing in the morning!"

A THIN-SKINNED SUSPECT

Silence on the other end of a 911 emergency call is a frightening experience for 911 dispatchers. It could mean anything; a victim unable to talk, an accidental dialing, or a silent plea for help. So when the Spartanburg Communications/911 Department received a 911 with no answer, they sent out police to investigate. When police entered the premises, they immediately found their culprit—a tomato. No, I'm not using Sam Spade vernacular here—it's not a woman I'm talking about—it's an actual tomato. Police surmised that the vine-ripened fruit fell from a basket situated above the phone and landed on the preset button for 911. Police grilled the tomato for a confession, then let it stew in its own juices. The tomato's lawyer says his client might fry for the offense.

REPORT . . . 911 REPORT . . . 911 REP
. 911 REPORT . . . 911 REPORT . . . 911
RT . . . 911 REPORT . . . 911 REPORT .
. 911 REPORT . . . 911 REPORT . . . 911
REPORT . . . 911 REPORT . . . 911 REP
. 911 REPORT . . . 911 REPORT . . . 911
REPORT . . . 911 REPORT . . . 911 REP
. 911 REPORT . . . 911 REPORT . . . 911

Man called to advise police that
aliens from Los Angeles were
tailing residents of Charlotte.

. 911 REPORT . . . 911 REPORT . . . 911
REPORT . . . 911 REPORT . . . 911 REP
. 911 REPORT . . . 911 REPORT . . . 911
REPORT . . . 911 REPORT . . . 911 REP
. 911 REPORT . . . 911 REPORT . . . 911

REPORT . . . 911 REPORT . . . 911 REP

OH, POOL BOY!

911: "911. Fire or emergency?"

CALLER: "Fire."

911: "Where's the fire, sir?"

CALLER: "No fire, really."

911: "Then what's the problem, sir?"

CALLER: "No real problem except it's so hot and the pump to our swimming pool is broken."

911: "Sir, do you have an emergency?"

CALLER: "Well, I was hoping that you could send the Fire Department out to fill our swimming pool."

THE ORIGIN OF SPECIES

"I didn't know what had me," said seventy-eight-year-old Edna Bradley about her terrible ordeal of August 24, 1992. The woman was hanging sheets on a clothesline when she was suddenly attacked from behind by an unknown assailant. She was knocked violently to the ground and was rolled around like a ball. Finally, she was able to get free and got a good look at her attacker. He was about four feet tall and very hairy—he was a chimpanzee who had escaped from the nearby Hollywild Animal Park. She and the chimp locked eyes, and that's when he came after her again.

"It grabbed me up again and rolled me over and over. I was just being rolled and tumbled every which way," Bradley said. The woman screamed for her daughter-in-law, who lives nearby, but nobody heard her. Bradley was finally able to break free, and she dashed into her house and called 911. When she looked through the back porch door, she could see the menacing yellow teeth of the chimp who was trying to get into her house. Finding no way in, the chimp finally loped away. Authorities discovered that three chimps had actually escaped from the animal park. One hijacked a mail carrier's car, forcing the postal employee out. The animals were recaptured by park owner David Meeks. In response to the monkey business she went through, Bradley said, "I tell you, it's a dangerous thing living beside a zoo."

REPORT . . . 911 REPORT . . . 911 REPO
. 911 REPORT . . . 911 REPORT . . . 911
RT . . . 911 REPORT . . . 911 REPORT .
. 911 REPORT . . . 911 REPORT . . . 911
REPORT . . . 911 REPORT . . . 911 REP
. 911 REPORT . . . 911 REPORT . . . 911
REPORT . . . 911 REPORT . . . 911 REP
. 911 RE "My dog is choking T . . . 911
REPORT or having a seizure. 911 REP
. 911 REPO What do I do?" ORT . . . 911
REPORT . . . 911 REPORT . . . 911 REP
. 911 REPORT . . . 911 REPORT . . . 911
REPORT . . . 911 REPORT . . . 911 REP
. 911 REPORT . . . 911 REPORT . . . 911
REPORT . . . 911 REPORT . . . 911 REP
. 911 REPORT . . . 911 REPORT . . . 911

96

REPORT . . . 911 REPORT . . . 911 REP

SCARED STRAIGHT

911: "911. Fire or emergency?"

CALLER: "A favor actually. I know you people, the police and all, are busy. But you've got to help me out."

911: "I'll do what I can. What's your emergency."

CALLER: "I was hoping you could send a policeman over here and have him scare my son into doing his homework."

911: "You want us to dispatch a policeman to frighten your son? Is that correct?"

CALLER: "Yeah, he won't do his homework, and I thought if a cop, uh, policeman, showed up and threatened to, like, take him to jail or something, my son might do his homework."

911: "I'm sorry, ma'am. We can't do that."

THE RAINBOW CONFRONTATION

911 DISPATCHER: "911. What's the nature of your emergency?"

CALLER: "You've got to help me out here. Now, I'm a good Christian woman and all, but this thing has gone too far."

911 DISPATCHER: "What are you talking about, ma'am?"

CALLER: "I love the Lord and I love all the people that love the Lord, but you might have to send me a policeman to get him out of my house."

911 DISPATCHER: "Is someone in your house?"

CALLER: "Yes, and he won't leave."

911 DISPATCHER: "Do you know who he is?"

CALLER: "I sure do. It's the Reverend Jesse Jackson, and he won't get off my couch."

IF YOUR FRIENDS TOLD
YOU TO JUMP OFF A BRIDGE . . .

He might have done it because he thought his luck had run out. But all that changed when an unidentified twenty-three-year-old man jumped off the San Francisco Bay Bridge in December 1995. How could that be a lucky thing? you might ask. Well, believe it or not, he landed next to a psychiatrist who happened to be in a rowboat at the time. Not only did the psychiatrist have a life jacket, he also had a cell phone. Dennis Tison, a law student as well as a psychiatrist, saw the man floating in the bay and tossed him his life jacket. Then he used the phone to dial 911.

"I just saw this head bobbing up, and I thought it was a sea lion, but it didn't go back under water," Tison said. "I asked him if he jumped from the bridge, and he said, 'Yes, get me out of here.'" The Coast Guard arrived within minutes and quickly pulled the jumper out of the water. Tison, who also had a camera with him, snapped pictures of the rescue. Since Tison is a psychiatrist, I wonder, Did he charge the jumper $80 for the session?

911 REPORT:

"My nail is broken."

SPECIAL DELIVERY

Palm Beach County Fire-Rescue dispatcher Jim English has helped nervous dads deliver before—but not one that was this nervous. At 1:49 A.M. on Wednesday, April 11, 1990, Richard LaMott dialed 911 and got English on the line. His wife was having a baby—right now!

DISPATCHER: "Fire-Rescue. Do you have an emergency?"

LAMOTT: "Yeah, I think we're going to have a baby."

DISPATCHER: "Okay, what's your . . . "

LAMOTT: "Right now!"

DISPATCHER: "Okay, hold on just a minute."

LAMOTT: "Oh, here it goes. Here it comes. You need to help me."

DISPATCHER: "Yes, I want you to get between the legs."

LAMOTT: "Yes, I'm right here. I see the baby."

DISPATCHER: "Okay, put your hands up there and catch the baby. Keep the baby from flopping out. . . . "

LAMOTT: "The baby's head is right here in front of me."

DISPATCHER: "Okay."

LAMOTT: "And it's stuck halfway and not coming any further."

DISPATCHER: "Okay, tell her to push."

LAMOTT: "Push babe, push. I see a face. Yeah, I see the face. It's starting to come."

DISPATCHER: "Tell her to keep pushing, keep breathing."

LaMott:	". . . There's blood around the baby's face."
Lori LaMott (in the background):	"Please God, don't let anything happen to my baby."
Dispatcher:	"Tell her to stay calm. She's got to breathe and push."
LaMott:	" . . . I don't hear no crying or nothing."
Dispatcher:	"Okay, we're gonna have to get the baby on out. She's gonna have to push."
LaMott:	"You have to push. Oh, here it comes. I'm delivering the baby. . . . "
Dispatcher:	"Support the baby. It's going to be slippery."

LAMOTT: "Holy . . . the baby's on the floor."

DISPATCHER: "Okay."

LAMOTT: "It's a boy, I think."

DISPATCHER: "Okay, we got to get the baby breathing."

LAMOTT: "He can't breathe. What do I got to do to clear his lungs?"

DISPATCHER: " . . . Is that the baby crying?"

LAMOTT: "Yeah, that's the baby crying."

"Just as I told dad, the baby was slippery. He found out the hard way," English said later. The baby girl, not a boy as the nervous father originally thought, was fine after her little bounce on the floor. By the end of the call, Jessica LaMott, five pounds six ounces, was nestled securely in her father's arms. The phone call and delivery lasted only four minutes.

HIS NAME WAS ART

Danny White, a real estate agent, was interested in a home in Columbus, Ohio, and went there with the home's owner, Mildred Sprouse. He was considering buying the house and fixing it up. While he was looking around, he noticed something on the floor, something that made him not want the house: a decomposing body. White ran out of the house and told Mildred what he had seen; she asked him not to call police. She explained that it was probably just some artwork. This didn't reassure White, and he grabbed his cell phone. Again, Mildred told White not to call police. She said her son Danny, who had been staying at the house, had a bad temper and wouldn't like it if he called police.

Well, a 911 phone call was made the next day, and police arrived anyway—even though White claims he didn't make the call. When police and paramedics arrived, it looked like they had a decomposing corpse on their hands all right. But there was one thing missing—that telltale stench of rotting flesh. "It had every appearance of being a severely decomposed body. It had the appearance of someone being there a long, long time," said Columbus EMS chief David Arrington.

It turned out to be a work of art called "Vietnam" by artist Dan Barfield. The work consisted of barbed wire and Barbie dolls burned with a blowtorch ("He hates Barbies," said Barfield's wife Judy). "It's certainly humorous now. I'm sure the medics were pleasantly surprised that it was wax," Arrington said. No autopsy was performed on the work of art, even though the coroner's office was initially called.

911 REPORT ... 911 REPORT ... 911 REPORT ... 911 REPORT ... 911 REPORT ... 911 REPORT ... 911 REPORT ... 911 REPORT ... 911 REPORT ... 911 REPORT ... 911 REPORT ... 911 REPORT ... 911 REPORT ... 911 REPORT ... 911 REPORT ... 911 REPORT ... 911 REPORT ... 911

Lady got blister from working three days at a Taco Bell.

911 REPORT ... 911 REPORT ... 911 REPORT ... 911 REPORT ... 911 REPORT ... 911 REPORT ... 911 REPORT ... 911 REPORT ... 911 REPORT ... 911 REPORT ... 911 REPORT ... 911 REPORT ... 911 REPORT ... 911 REPORT ... 911 REPORT ... 911

FRAZZLED CALLER

911 OPERATOR: "911. What's your emergency?"

FEMALE: "Yes, I need the police to come and pick me up, please."

911 OPERATOR: "Are you in trouble? Do you have an emergency?"

FEMALE: "I just had my hair done."

911 OPERATOR: "I'm sorry . . . "

FEMALE: "I need a policeman to come and take me home. Because it's raining and I rode my bike to the store. I need them to take me home, or my hair will get wet."

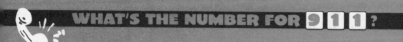

BUMPER BAMBI

DISPATCHER: "911."

CALLER: "I'm reporting a deer on the road. I almost hit it."

DISPATCHER: "Is the deer alive?"

CALLER: "Oh, no, it's run over. Many, many cars. Again and again, and—*Oh, no!!! Not again!*"

IT WASN'T THE HAIR OF THE DOG THAT BIT THEM

Two men, Joe Buddy Caine of Edwardsville, Alabama, and his friend Junior Bright, had been drinking when they came across a four-foot rattlesnake. So they did what anyone would do—they picked it up and started tossing it to each another. And the snake did what any snake would do—it bit Bright on the hand and then, when Caine tried to kill it, bit him on the arm. The two men called 911. When paramedics arrived, both were in a semiconscious state (although it seems to me that they were in a semiconscious state to begin with). Caine went into cardiac arrest on the ambulance ride to the hospital and died about an hour after being bitten. From these two men, we've all learned a valuable lesson: Don't drink and toss snakes!

911 REPORT:

"What do I do if a tornado hits?"

YOU LEAVE ME . . . BREATHLESS

DISPATCHER: "911. Fire or emergency?"

WOMAN: "Uh, I got a girl here who's having a hard time breathing."

DISPATCHER: "How old is she?"

WOMAN: "About twenty-one, twenty-two, something like that."

DISPATCHER: "Is she conscious?"

WOMAN: "Yeah, she's just lying here looking around and breathing real hard."

DISPATCHER: "Do you know if she's an asthmatic?"

WOMAN: "Not that I know of."

DISPATCHER: "Have someone check her purse for an inhaler."

WOMAN: "Sure." *(Calls to someone to check purse.)* "She's a member of the club here, and it's never happened before."

DISPATCHER: "What was she doing right before the attack?"

WOMAN: "Uh, she was dancing."

DISPATCHER: "Has her breathing normalized any?"

WOMAN: "No, she's still struggling and wheezing."

DISPATCHER: "Try loosening her clothes to make her more comfortable."

WOMAN: "I don't think that would help."

DISPATCHER: "Why not?"

WOMAN: "Like I said, she's a dancer."

DISPATCHER: "Yes . . . "

WOMAN: "She works over here at the Pleasure Chest—she's a topless dancer, you know."

DISPATCHER: "Oh . . . "

A SNAPPY REACTION

Portland, Oregon, police and firefighters were dispatched by a 911 call to check on a five-year-old boy who had been attacked by an animal. These calls can be quit an ordeal: a crying, bleeding child; an animal that has to be hunted down and possibly destroyed; frightened parents. When fireman Hal Westberg arrived on the scene, he realized the situation wasn't as dramatic as all that. A young boy had stuck his tongue out at his pet turtle who responded by chomping down on the boy's tongue and not letting go. The turtle stayed latched on for fifteen minutes until officials showed up. Westberg said he simply slipped his pen in the turtle's mouth, added a little pressure, and the turtle let go. The young boy didn't require medical attention. As for the turtle—he was transferred to a minimum security tank at a relative's house.

REPORT ... 911 REPORT ... 911 REPORT ... 911 REPORT ... 911 REPORT ... 911

REPORT ... 911 REPORT ... 911 REPORT ... 911 REPORT ... 911 REPORT ... 911

REPORT ... 911 REPORT ... 911 REPORT ... 911 REPORT ... 911 REPORT ... 911 REPORT ... 911 REPORT ... 911 REPORT ... 911

Complainant, a small boy, called to report that his bird had run out of birdseed.

REPORT ... 911 REPORT ... 911 REPORT ... 911 REPORT ... 911 REPORT ... 911 REPORT ... 911 REPORT ... 911 REPORT ... 911 REPORT ... 911 REPORT ... 911

CHAIN OF FOOLS

DISPATCHER: "911. Fire or emergency?"

MAN: "Fire, I guess."

DISPATCHER: "How can I help you, sir?"

MAN: "I was wondering . . . uh, does the Fire Department put snow chains on their trucks?"

DISPATCHER: "Yes, sir. Do you have an emergency?"

MAN: "Well, you know, the snow's been pretty bad here lately."

DISPATCHER: "Yes sir, I'm aware of that."

MAN: "It's just . . . well, I've spent the last four hours trying to put these darn chains on my tires and I . . . it's just . . . well, do you think once the Fire Department has their chains on, they could come over and help me?"

DISPATCHER: "Help you what, sir?"

MAN: "Help me get these damn chains on my car!"

911 REPORT . . . 911 REPORT . . . 911 REPO
. 911 REPORT . . . 911 REPORT . . . 911
REPORT . . . 911 REPORT . . . 911 REPO
. 911 REPORT . . . 911 REPORT . . . 911
REPORT . . . 911 REPORT . . . 911 REPO
. 911 REPORT . . . 911 REPORT . . . 911
REPORT . . . 911 REPORT . . . 911 REPO

911 "I want an officer to come 911
REPORT out and take care of a 911 REPO
911 REP low-flying aircraft."T . . . 911
REPORT . . . 911 REPORT . . . 911 REPO
911 REPORT . . . 911 REPORT . . . 911
REPORT . . . 911 REPORT . . . 911 REPO
911 REPORT . . . 911 REPORT . . . 911
REPORT . . . 911 REPORT . . . 911 REPO
911 REPORT . . . 911 REPORT . . . 911

REPORT . . . 911 REPORT . . . 911 REPO

SORRY, I'M ALL
TIED UP AT THE MOMENT

A woman who was helping her cousin do janitorial work at the Booby Trap strip club in Pompano Beach, Florida, became an overnight celebrity. Two men wearing ski masks slipped in through an unlocked door after the club closed on September 28, 1998, and tied up the two janitors. They put one woman in the men's bathroom and left the other one in the front—making sure they were both securely tied up—and then placed a piece of tape over their eyes. The armed gunmen then stole a refrigerator-size safe containing more than $50,000 in cash and left.

From the corner of her eye and through a small opening in the tape, the woman in the men's room could see a pay phone on the wall. She nudged the receiver off the hook and dialed 911 with her tongue. Not knowing if the robbers were still in the building and unable to hear if a dispatcher was actually on the line, the woman carefully whispered "Help. Help."

She could hear her cousin calling from the next room, so she inched along, following the sound of her voice until they were near each other. The woman bent down near her cousin's hands, and the cousin was able to remove the tape from her eyes. She then went behind the bar, found another phone, and again dialed 911 with her tongue. Police arrived at the Booby Trap and freed the two women. It's a good thing she wasn't tongue-tied.

IT'S YOUR OWN ASPHALT

911 DISPATCHER: "911. What's your emergency?"

MAN: "Yes, can you tell me what the hell is going on on 55?"

911 DISPATCHER: "I'm sorry sir. Is there an emergency you wish to report?"

MAN: "Look, traffic hasn't moved in fifteen minutes—what the hell is the problem?"

911: "Sir, this is the emergency number . . . "

MAN: "Yes, yes, yes, I know that—but I'm in a hurry. Is there another way to get to Central from here?"

DIAL A DATE

When you call 911, you expect to get prompt, professional service—but not a dating service. Unfortunately, that's exactly what happened in Daytona Beach, Florida, when Joey Winn called 911 in July 1998 to report that her Ormond Beach mobile home had been burglarized. The call was answered by Steve Toncheff of the Volusia County Sheriff's Office. Toncheff took Winn's information and dispatched a deputy to the scene.

About twenty minutes later, Toncheff called Winn back to follow up and see how she was doing. "He said he knew it was inappropriate and said he had never done this before, but would I like to go out sometime," Ms. Winn said.

The two dated for about three weeks until the *News-Journal* of Daytona Beach broke the story. It was then uncovered that Toncheff had used Sheriff's Office computers to get personal information about women who had called to report emergencies. Toncheff was suspended from his job. Was he bachelor number one, bachelor number two, or bachelor number three?

911 REPORT:

"Eighteen-year-old male couldn't get any rest at home and wanted a ride to the hospital."

BRIDGE OVER TROUBLED WATER

In December 1990, the old Mercer Island bridge in Seattle, Washington, began breaking up because of high floodwaters. It was a pretty unbelievable sight—especially for the 911 operators who only heard about it but didn't see it.

FIRST CALL

CALLER: "This may sound silly, but have you received any report that the I-90, the old bridge, may be sinking? I just drove by it, and the midsection, the old section they are working on, appears to be awfully low in the water."

OPERATOR: "Gee . . . no, we haven't . . . ahhhh . . . uhhh . . ."

CALLER: "I'm just wondering if there might be some storm damage. It takes an awful lot of water to bring it that far down. I though someone might want to take a look at it."

OPERATOR: Yeah . . . I'll let the Department of Transportation know, and they can check it out."

CALLER: "Okay, I drove by there about 9:15, and it was sitting pretty low. There was a definite dip to it."

NEXT CALL

CALLER: "This is Seattle Fire. You guys don't have any info on the old bridge right now, do you?"

OPERATOR
(laughs): "I'm trying to get hold of the Department of Transportation. Some guy just called and said he thinks it's sinking."

CALLER: "It is sinking."

OPERATOR: "It *is* sinking???"

CALLER: "Just got a call from a guy on the bridge who's the contractor, who says their pumps failed, and they got water to the top of the bridge right now, midspan."

OPERATOR: "Oh lovely . . . "

NEXT CALL

CALLER: "I know you are probably aware, but the floating bridge has broken in two."

OPERATOR
(in disbelief):   "It's now broken in two?"

CALLER: "Yes. It's floating south."

OPERATOR: "OK. Great. We are on our way."

NEXT CALL

CALLER: "We just drove across I-90, and the midspan of the old bridge . . . "

OPERATOR: "Yeah. We've already got that, and we are on our way."

CALLER: "OK . . . Well, can you tell me what happened?"

OPERATOR: "Can you hold? We are kind of in a state of emergency here."

I CAN'T TAKE IT ANYMORE!!!

Suspected bank robber Leroy Tucker was tired of his life on the run. He decided to give himself up. Tucker called 911 and turned himself in on the same day he robbed the Hospital Trust National Bank in Cranston, Rhode Island. In fact, Tucker was only about a mile away from the bank when he made the call from a pay phone. Withdrawn, returned—taken out of circulation.

911 REPORT

Dispatcher to police: "Male caller says a light in the breezeway of his apartment building has been broken out. Wants police to change it."

RUNAWAY CALLER

911 DISPATCHER: "911."

MAN: "Yeah, I'm having trouble breathing. I'm all out of breath. Damn . . . I think I'm going to pass out."

911 DISPATCHER: "Sir, where are you calling from?"

MAN: "I'm at a pay phone. North and Foster. Damn . . . "

911 DISPATCHER: "Sir, an ambulance is on the way. Are you an asthmatic?"

MAN: "No . . . "

911 DISPATCHER: "What were you doing before you started having trouble breathing?"

MAN: "Running from the police . . . "

THERE WAS A CROOKED MAN . . .

911: "911 Emergency."

MAN: "Yeah, I got's me a problem."

911: "What's your problem, sir?"

MAN: "They's something wrong with my teeth."

911: "With your teeth, sir?"

MAN: "Yeah, my teeth. I got these false teeth here, and they don't fit right in my mouth. They're all crooked in my mouth, don't you know."

911: "Sir, 911 is for emergencies only."

MAN: "I know that and I'm sorry about that. To me, see, this here is an emergency. I need to get my teeth fixed, see. I can't be going to church until someone comes down here and fixes my teeth for me."

I HATE IT WHEN THAT HAPPENS

A man heard his neighbor shouting and screaming in pain and immediately called 911. When paramedics arrived, no one answered the door, but they could hear the man in obvious distress yelling from the back room. They banged on the door, and the man suddenly yelled that he was all right and didn't need their help. The emergency team realized something was wrong and broke down the door and entered the man's house.

They found the man in the bathroom and immediately realized why he was screaming in pain but still didn't want anyone to help—his penis had become lodged in the bathroom sink drain. The man explained that he was changing a lightbulb above the sink when he slipped and fell. Miraculously, his penis lodged in the drain and swelled to such an extent that the man couldn't remove it. Paramedics administered an injection which cause the swelling to recede so that the man's penis could be pulled out of the drain.

Just in case you're wondering—the sink suffered no permanent damage.

REPORT . . . 911 REPORT . . . 911 REPC
911 REPORT . . . 911 REPORT . . . 911
REPORT . . . 911 REPORT . . . 911 REPC
911 REPORT . . . 911 REPORT . . . 911
REPORT . . . 911 REPORT . . . 911 REPC
911 REPORT . . . 911 REPORT . . . 911
REPORT . . . 911 REPORT . . . 911 REPC
911 REPORT . . . 911 REPORT . . . 911

"Yeah, my cable's out. Can you
send someone around?"

REPORT . . . 911 REPORT . . . 911 REPC
911 REPORT . . . 911 REPORT . . . 911
REPORT . . . 911 REPORT . . . 911 REPC
911 REPORT . . . 911 REPORT . . . 911
REPORT . . . 911 REPORT . . . 911 REPC
911 REPORT . . . 911 REPORT . . . 911

REPORT . . . 911 REPORT . . . 911 REP

PLOWED OVER

911 DISPATCHER: "911."

CALLER: "Yeah, hey. There's a snowplow that's working Biltmore, right?"

911 DISPATCHER: "I wouldn't know that, sir."

CALLER: "Okay, well, there is. Anyways, how 'bout doing me a favor and getting that guy on the plow to come down my street here and clear the snow?"

911 DISPATCHER: "I'm sorry, sir. I can't do that."

CALLER: "Come on. I know all about you 911 people—I know you guys got pull. Do me a favor, will ya?"

BRING HOME THE BACON

When the 911 emergency dispatcher answered the call, all she heard were huffs and puffs. Sounded to the dispatcher like it was a woman in distress, and she called in a rescue squad to go to the residence. When the rescue team arrived, they found a woman all right—but she was peacefully watching television. There was no problem. No emergency. So who made the call? It turned out to be Juliet. Juliet was the woman's roommate. She was also a real pig—a twenty-five-pound Vietnamese pot-bellied pig to be exact. Apparently Juliet had knocked the phone off the hook and hit the automatic dial button for 911—then just breathed and snorted when the dispatcher answered the call. "I really feel bad about putting the Fire Department through all that," the woman said. "I really appreciate all the work they did." The pig's owner finally confessed that this wasn't Juliet's first incident involving the telephone. The pig once ate a phone book, she said.

REPORT ... 911 REPORT ... 911 REP
. 911 REPORT ... 911 REPORT ... 91
RT ... 911 REPORT ... 911 REPORT .
. 911 REPORT ... 911 REPORT ... 91
REPORT ... 911 REPORT ... 911 REP
. 911 REPORT ... 911 REPORT ... 91
REPORT ... 911 REPORT ... 911 REP

Woman called three times
to report UFOs are coming to
mechanize her brain.

REPORT ... 911 REPORT ... 911 REP
. 911 REPORT ... 911 REPORT ... 91
REPORT ... 911 REPORT ... 911 REP
. 911 REPORT ... 911 REPORT ... 91
REPORT ... 911 REPORT ... 911 REP
. 911 REPORT ... 911 REPORT ... 91

REPORT ... 911 REPORT ... 911 REP

GOT MILK?

DISPATCHER:	"911"
CALLER:	"I need an ambulance to take me to the hospital."
DISPATCHER:	"What is the problem, ma'am?"
CALLER:	"My breasts are not lactating."
DISPATCHER *(very dumbfounded)*:	"Excuse me . . . ?"
CALLER:	"I gave birth twelve days ago, and my breasts are not lactating."

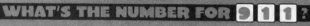
UNCLEAR RECEPTION

911 DISPATCHER: "911."

MAN: "Yeah, my television don't work right."

911 DISPATCHER: "Sir, you've called 911."

MAN: "That's right, 'cause the TV in my room . . . the picture's not too good. Could you send someone to fix it?"

911 DISPATCHER: "Sir, are you calling from your home?"

MAN: "No. I'm in room 32—I'm sharing it with some other fellow. I just want to watch some TV."

911 DISPATCHER: "Sir, you need to call someone at the hospital. 911 is for emergencies only."

MAN: "Oh. Could you connect me to the nurses' station?"

HE'S GOT A TICKET TO RIDE

An elderly man in Houston called 911 and reported that he was having difficulty breathing. Two Houston Fire Department paramedics were dispatched to his residence with full gear. When they arrived, they discovered the man sitting on the steps of his home smoking a cigarette, a packed suitcase on the stoop beside him. He told the stunned paramedics that he had an appointment at the Veterans Administration Hospital. Could they give him a ride, as he had no other way of getting there? The man told the paramedics where he wanted to go—I wonder if the paramedics told the man where they would like him to go?

911 REPORT:

Caller: "Is it okay for a civilian to take a person to the hospital, or does the ambulance have to do it?"

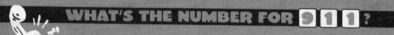

HOME DELIVERY

911: "911."

WOMAN: "Thank God."

911: "Do you have an emergency?"

WOMAN: "What a day, let me tell you. I had planned on finishing all my Christmas shopping today when my boss called and told me he needed me to pull the Master's report from my computer and drop it by his office. Well, I did, and of course, he complained about a couple of things, so I had to trudge back to my office and make a whole series of corrections and changes, reprint it, and bring it back to him. I rushed to Marshal's to finish up my shopping and had to stand in line with thousands of other people, and of course, the woman in front of me needed price checks on everything—and I mean everything. Finally, I get checked out and get all the presents in my car and realize that if I'm lucky I'll be able to beat the kids home from school. So I'm driving down the street and the idiot in front of me decides to stop for no reason and I have to swerve so I don't hit him and I wind up in the ditch and can't get out. Well, thank God I'm not hurt, and the car and the presents are okay, so I climb out of the car and climb up the hill, which wasn't easy 'cause it's covered with ice and snow, but fortunately I was only a couple of blocks from my house, so I called my neighbor, Joan, and she came and picked me up, thank God. I get home and call the towing company, and can you believe it? They said they wouldn't be able to tow my car for ten to twelve hours. Ten to twelve hours!"

911: "Ma'am, are you injured?"

WOMAN: "No, but all my Christmas presents are still in the car, and I need you to send a police officer to my car and have him get all the gifts out of the car and bring them to my home."

911: "I'm sorry, ma'am, but we don't have the manpower or resources to send out an officer. This line is for emergencies only."

WOMAN: "Great! Perfect ending to my day! I've never called you people before, have I? No. I can't believe the taxes I pay that you people can't help me out in my moment of need!"

911: "I'm sorry, ma'am."

WOMAN: "Well, you'd better hope that Santa picks them up for me . . . that's all I can say!"

BREAKING IN LINE

The guilt must have been more than he could bear—or maybe he just had indigestion. Police responding to a 911 hang-up from the Conejo Valley Montessori School in Thousand Oaks, California, discovered suspected burglar Doug Mattson waiting for them. When deputies arrived, they entered through an open door and discovered Mattson eating a piece of pie. Police also discovered that he had apparently eaten a cupcake. Someone breaking into a school to eat cafeteria food? Now, that's a first.

911 REPORT:

A six-year-old called 911 because his
brother took one of his toys.

RIM SHOT

911: "Fire and Ambulance."

CALLER: "Yes sir, I need an ambulance for my son. He has his finger stuck in a Hot Wheels car."

911: "I'm sorry, sir. Is this an emergency?"

CALLER: "Well, it's his favorite one!"

COOCHIE, COOCHIE, COO

911: "911."

CALLER: "I'm having a baby!"

911: "All right. Stay calm, ma'am."

CALLER: "I'm calm. I'm just having a baby! Now!"

911: "How far apart are the contractions?"

CALLER: "They seem like they're coming right on top of each other."

911: "Has your water broke?"

CALLER: "Yeah, my water broke about a half-hour ago. That's when the contractions starting hitting real hard."

911: "Can you see if the baby is crowning?"

CALLER: "What?"

911: "Look and see if you can see the top of the baby's head."

CALLER: "I can't do that."

911: "Why not?"

CALLER: "I still have my clothes on."

911: "Ma'am, the paramedics are on their way, so there's no need to worry. I need for you to remove all of your clothing from the waist down so that you can check to see if you're crowning."

CALLER: "I ain't gonna do that! I don't want them boys [paramedics] to see my coochie."

REPORT . . . 911 REPORT . . . 911 REP
. 911 REPORT . . . 911 REPORT . . . 911
RT . . . 911 REPORT . . . 911 REPORT .
. 911 REPORT . . . 911 REPORT . . . 911
REPORT . . . 911 REPORT . . . 911 REP
. 911 REPORT . . . 911 REPORT . . . 911
REPORT . . . 911 REPORT . . . 911 REP
. 911 RE Complainant called T . . . 911
REPOR about neighbor keeping 11 REP
. 911 RE a pet cow in the yard. T . . . 911
REPORT . . . 911 REPORT . . . 911 REP
. 911 REPORT . . . 911 REPORT . . . 911
REPORT . . . 911 REPORT . . . 911 REP
. 911 REPORT . . . 911 REPORT . . . 911
REPORT . . . 911 REPORT . . . 911 REP
. 911 REPORT . . . 911 REPORT . . . 911

REPORT . . . 911 REPORT . . . 911 REP

IT'S JUST THE FAX, MA'AM

Karl Gutknecht, public affairs director for the Wisconsin Agriculture Department, placed a document in his fax machine, keyed in the phone number, and left the machine unattended. "I just missed it by one digit," says Gutknecht, who was trying to dial 919, an area code in North Carolina. "I thought I dialed 919. Then I left it and went to the bathroom. It apparently dialed 911 quite a few times." Office manager Sue Buroker answered the call from the Dane County Sheriff's Office questioning the repeated 911 calls. She told officials the fax machine had been under a lot of stress. Gutknecht remarked of the incident, "It's a good reminder to me to slow down—or next time it will be 911." It wasn't an emergency phone call—it wasn't even a reasonable facsimile.

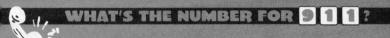

AN EMERGENCY DRILL

AKRON 911: "What is your emergency?"

MAN: "I've had a toothache since yesterday. My tooth is all swelled up. I'd like to go to St. Thomas for medication."

911: "Sir, is this an emergency?"

MAN: "Well, it sure hurts like hell!"

IT'S NINE O'CLOCK.
DO YOU KNOW WHERE
YOUR CHILDREN ARE?

A six-year-old boy, whose name was not released, awoke from a nap at the Loving Care Child Care Center in North Memphis to find himself totally alone. It was 8:43 P.M., and apparently, the child had been overlooked when the facility closed for the day. Was he frightened? Did he panic? Nope—he called 911. He told the dispatcher "everybody's gone." The facility offers both day and nighttime care—the boy was found on the day care side. The boy's mother picked up the child at 10 P.M. that night. Let's see. It's a day care center, but no one missed the boy until 8:43 at night—and he's the one who called 911?

911 REPORT:

"My dog is stuck under the house."

WHAT IS 9 PLUS 1 PLUS 1?

DISPATCHER: "911."

CHILD: "Uh, can you help me with my math homework?"

DISPATCHER: "Son, you've called the emergency number."

CHILD: "Yeah, I know. This is an emergency."

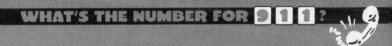

CLOTHES MINDED

911: "911. What's your emergency?"

WOMAN: "I heard what sounded like gunshots coming from the brown house on the corner here."

911: "Do you have an address?"

WOMAN: "No, I'm wearing a blouse and slacks. Why?"

911 REPORT ... 911 REPORT ... 911 REP
. 911 REPORT ... 911 REPORT ... 911
RT ... 911 REPORT ... 911 REPORT .
. 911 REPORT ... 911 REPORT ... 911
REPORT ... 911 REPORT ... 911 REP
. 911 REPORT ... 911 REPORT ... 911
REPORT ... 911 REPORT ... 911 REP

"My toilet is plugged.
I want you to send someone
out to fix it."

REPORT ... 911 REPORT ... 911 REP
. 911 REPORT ... 911 REPORT ... 911
REPORT ... 911 REPORT ... 911 REP
. 911 REPORT ... 911 REPORT ... 911
REPORT ... 911 REPORT ... 911 REP
. 911 REPORT ... 911 REPORT ... 911

REPORT ... 911 REPORT ... 911 REP

THERE'S A FIRST TIME FOR EVERYTHING

It was Jerry Duplantis's first day on the job in January 1991—and the first day that Houma, Louisiana, had implemented the 911 emergency service. The cheering cry "It works!" was heard when the first phone call came in over the new equipment. Duplantis got the first call.

"I got the call, and a boy was hollering, '302 Mike St. is on fire!'" said Duplantis. "I said, 'That's my house.'" The call was from Duplantis's eleven-year-old son. Bayou Cane Fire Department volunteers were extinguishing the blaze a short three minutes after the boy's call.

"My biggest concern was for my kids," Duplantis said. An ambulance driver phoned Duplantis to let him know both his boys, Corey and Casey, were fine but his rented home had suffered some fire damage. At least the kids didn't have to ask their father "What did you do at work today, dad?"

A CRUSHING PROBLEM

911 DISPATCHER: "911. Fire or emergency?"

CALLER: "It's an emergency."

911 DISPATCHER: "How can I help you, sir?"

CALLER: "I'll tell you how you can damn-well help me. You can call that g—d— hospital across the street and tell them to shut the hell up."

911 DISPATCHER: "Is there a disturbance at . . . "

CALLER: "The Christ Memorial hospital—across the damn street here. They're making a racket and I can't g—d— sleep."

911 DISPATCHER: "What's going on there, sir?"

CALLER: "Just send a policeman over there, or you call them, and tell them to shut off their kidney-stone crusher. That things been going all night, and I've got to get me some g—d— sleep!"

THIS IS ONLY A TEST

911 DISPATCHER: "York County emergency."

WOMAN: "Yes, what is all that racket?"

911 DISPATCHER: "Ma'am?"

WOMAN: "Those sirens . . . they've been going on for hours it seems."

911 DISPATCHER: "Those are warning sirens, ma'am. There's high winds that could easily turn into a tornado. We wanted people to be prepared."

WOMAN: "Well, that's just fine. But they're hurting my dog's ears, and I want you to turn them off."

SMOKE 'EM IF YOU GOT 'EM

A fifty-seven-year-old man, Milton Trautman, was released on bond with the condition that he never use the emergency 911 number unless it is an actual emergency. The Madison, Wisconsin, man had called 911 while suffering from a nicotine fit—he asked the dispatcher if they could deliver cigarettes to his home.

911 REPORT:

"When does the Burger King open?"
(The caller did not specify which Burger King.)

911 REPORT ... 911 REPORT ... 911 REPORT ... 911 REPORT ... 911 REPORT ... 911 REPORT ... 911 REPORT ... 911 REPORT ... 911 REPORT ... 911 REPORT ... 911 REPORT ... 911 REPORT ... 911 REPORT ... 911

"Why is the sun
so hot in Arizona?"

CALLER GETS COLLECTED

An obscene caller decided to give someone a ring and whisper sweet nothings into his or her ear. Too bad for this horny half-wit that he chose to call 911 to express himself. Unbeknownst to the dirty dialer, the 911 system in Nassau County, New York, was "enhanced," which means the caller's address and phone number appeared on the computer screen. Even though the caller might not have called for sexual gratification, he did wind up fingering himself.

WHEN THE BOUGH BREAKS

911: "911. Fire or emergency?"

CALLER: "Now, I've called about this before, and you people didn't do anything about it. Now they're back, and I'm getting a little sick and tired of it."

911: "What's going on, ma'am?"

CALLER: "I just think it's the most sickening thing I've ever seen. And I wish you people would do something about it. It's those statue people. They're doing it again. The statue people are having sex in my trees."

CREATURE COMFORTS

911: "911."

CALLER: "Yes, hello. I'm sorry to bother you. Could you do me a favor, young lady?"

911: "Yes, ma'am, if I can."

CALLER: "Good. You see, my kitty, Tex, died a few days ago. Poor little thing—I had to put him to sleep. It was pitiful."

911: "I'm sorry to hear that, ma'am."

CALLER: "Thank you, dear. That's very sweet. But now Tiny is very depressed . . . just moping around, won't eat . . . cries all the time."

911: "Tiny?"

CALLER: "Tex's sister."

911: "How can I help you?"

CALLER: "I was wondering if you could send over a policeman to help me console little Tiny. I don't know what to do for the poor thing."

OFF ITS CRADLE

Raymond Herzog of Syracuse, New York, was sleeping peacefully when suddenly there came a loud knocking at his front door. Herzog was surprised to find a police officer who said he was responding to an emergency 911 call that was traced to "this" address. There was a tense moment when Herzog wondered if someone was with him in the house. He let the police officer in to investigate. It turned out that the phone call was made by—the phone. That is, the phone itself made the call. According to an AT&T spokesman, cordless phones more than five years old can accidentally call 911 by themselves because frequencies from the air can emit pitches that the phone registers as 9 and 1. I don't think that's what "auto-dial" is supposed to mean.

REPORT . . . 911 REPORT . . . 911 REP
. 911 REPORT . . . 911 REPORT . . . 911
RT . . . 911 REPORT . . . 911 REPORT .
. 911 REPORT . . . 911 REPORT . . . 911
REPORT . . . 911 REPORT . . . 911 REP
. 911 REPORT . . . 911 REPORT . . . 911
REPORT . . . 911 REPORT . . . 911 REP

"Yeah, hi. I was wondering if
you could tell me how bad the
snow is in Queen City?"

REPORT . . . 911 REPORT . . . 911 REP
. 911 REPORT . . . 911 REPORT . . . 911
REPORT . . . 911 REPORT . . . 911 REP
. 911 REPORT . . . 911 REPORT . . . 911
REPORT . . . 911 REPORT . . . 911 REP
. 911 REPORT . . . 911 REPORT . . . 911

REPORT . . . 911 REPORT . . . 911 REP

HERE'S JOHNNY!

DISPATCHER: "911. Fire or emergency?"

WOMAN
(whispering): "Help me . . . there's someone in my house."

DISPATCHER: "Where are you now, ma'am?"

WOMAN: "I'm hiding under the bed. Oh, God, someone's coming down the hall. Help . . . quick."

DISPATCHER: "Just remain calm and stay on the line."

WOMAN: "Hurry, hurry."

DISPATCHER: "Officers are on the way, ma'am."

WOMAN: "He's trying to get in the door. Please help. Oh, God."

MAN'S VOICE
(muffled): "Joan! Joan, are you in there?"

WOMAN: "Bill? Never mind, it's just my husband."

A REAL TURKEY OF A PHONE CALL

911: "911."

CALLER: "Hi, is this the police?"

911: "This is 911. Do you need police assistance?"

CALLER: "Well, I was wondering. I don't know who to call. Can you tell me how to cook a turkey? I've never cooked one before."

CALLING BIG BIRD

From a single pay phone in Jersey City, New Jersey, more than four hundred 911 calls were made within one year. Unfortunately, every one of them was a fake and a prank. Police were tired and frustrated with the naughty 911 caller and decided to stake out the pay phone and catch the criminal red-fingered. Imagine their surprise when a little six-year-old girl, who could barely reach the phone, turned out to be their hardened criminal. The girl, whose parents have agreed to take her to a crisis-intervention counselor to help her realize the importance of 911 calls, made every one of the 400 calls. She reached her apex in March 1995 with 130 calls in that month alone and had made 9 calls in one and a half hours on the Sunday before her arrest. Maybe she was trying to call the new preteen rock group, "911."

911 REPORT:

Young Caller: "Hi, I just swallowed a penny. Am I going to die?"

FLOAT LIKE A BUTTERFLY . . .

DISPATCHER: "Sheriff's Department."

MALE CALLER: "Yeah, there's this big sting operation going on all around me, and I know you guys know about it, and I want you to know this is not a part of me. I know cops are following me and I didn't know about this until you guys started your twenty-four-hour surveillance three or four days ago. I want you to know it's not me. Me and my girlfriend are not a part of it."

DISPATCHER: "Sir, I don't know anything about any sting operation."

CALLER: "I just want you to know it's not me, OK? Me and my girlfriend, we're not a part of it."

DISPATCHER: "OK." *(Hangs up.)*

NEXT CALL

DISPATCHER: "Sheriff's Department."

SAME CALLER: "Yeah, I want you to know me and my girlfriend are renting here, and now these guys are trying to throw us out because of this [alleged surveillance]. It's a real big inconvenience for us, so could you hurry up and finish it before the end of the month?"

DISPATCHER: "OK."

NOT QUITE A LOVE NOTE

William Randall fell asleep while watching the Indianapolis 500 on February 17, 1991, and when he woke up, he had a terrible migraine headache. His wife, Roberta, had left to wash the car and go shopping. When she returned home, she found William shivering, pale, bleeding, and unable to stand.

He complained about the headache for three days without doing anything about it. "To the best of my recollection, I am not sure what happened. I kept throwing up blood and crawling around on my stomach," said Randall. Finally, after speaking to his employer, Randall went to the hospital, where doctors found a .25-caliber bullet lodged in the back of his head.

Investigators found the following note, in Roberta Randall's handwriting: "Honey, you have been shot in the face. Call 911. I am so sorry. I love you so much." Police quickly uncovered the fact that Roberta had shot her husband of eight years in the face while he slept and

then gone out to run errands. "I knew I had to do it. I know I shot him. I just don't remember. My mind and body were somehow separated," said Roberta in a probation report, later telling probation officials she felt "bored and sad" the day of the shooting.

Her husband, who lost sight in his left eye from the gunshot wound, said, "At first I did want to prosecute, but now I don't. As good as we were together, I just can't believe this." William Randall told investigators the only reason he could think of why his wife would shoot him is that he bets on his golf games. Roberta was sentenced to five years for the shooting but not before pleading for leniency by saying, "I beg for probation. Bill needs me." If someone asked Roberta if she would consider reconciling with her husband after her release, I wonder if she would say, "I'll take another shot at it."

911 REPORT:

"I just saw a coyote in the greenbelt near Highlands Ranch."

ADDRESS UNKNOWN

911: "911. Fire or police?"

CALLER: "Yeah. Well, police, I guess. Someone stole my mailbox."

911: "Can I have your address, sir?"

CALLER: "It's gone."

TAKING A BITE OUT OF CRIME

911: "911. What's your emergency?"

WOMAN: "Someone broke into my house and took a bite out of my ham-and-cheese sandwich."

911: "Excuse me?"

WOMAN: "I made a ham-and-cheese sandwich and left it on the kitchen table, and when I came back from the bathroom, someone had taken a bite out of it."

911: "Was anything else taken?"

WOMAN: "No. But this has happened to me before, you know, and I'm sick and tired of it."

INSTANT JUSTICE

A twenty-year-old woman from Tucson, Arizona, Linda Martinez, was angry with the police for arresting her on vandalism charges. And to prove how mad she was, she set about slashing twenty-four tires on six police cars parked outside the police station. On the last tire, the knife slipped a little, and Martinez cut a huge gash in her hand. "She cut her hands with the butcher knife she used to slash the tires and called 911," said an unidentified police officer. "This gets dumber. She told the operator she cut her hands while slashing 'the tires on your [expletive] cars.'" Paramedics treated Martinez at the scene of the tire slashing. She was arrested after the treatment but released on her own recognizance.

REPORT . . . 911 REPORT . . . 911 REP
. 911 REPORT . . . 911 REPORT . . . 911
REPORT . . . 911 REPORT . . . 911 REP
. 911 REPORT . . . 911 REPORT . . . 911
REPORT . . . 911 REPORT . . . 911 REP
. 911 REPORT . . . 911 REPORT . . . 911
REPORT . . . 911 REPORT . . . 911 REP

"Did we just have an
earthquake? Where was is
centered? How strong was it?
What was the damage?"

. 911 REPORT . . . 911 REPORT . . . 911
REPORT . . . 911 REPORT . . . 911 REP
. 911 REPORT . . . 911 REPORT . . . 911
REPORT . . . 911 REPORT . . . 911 REP
. 911 REPORT . . . 911 REPORT . . . 911
REPORT . . . 911 REPORT . . . 911 REP

167

YOU BIG BABY!

911: "911."

WOMAN: "My baby's been shot! My baby's been shot!"

Paramedics were dispatched immediately. They reported back that the woman's "baby" was a thirty-one-year-old man.

THE ONE THAT GOT AWAY

DISPATCHER: "Sheriff's Department."

MALE CALLER: "Yeah, there's this commercial fishing boat that's been circling Cayucos Pier. It goes up . . . and around . . . and ain't nobody caught nothin' today. I pay an outrageous price to fish in the waters of California, and the fishin's not that great out here as it is, you know what I mean, to have this guy out here. I don't want you to do anything. I just wanted you to know."

I'VE GOT BLISTERS ON MY FINGERS!

He's someone with too much time on his hands and too many phones at his disposal. Police and the Federal Communications Commission used special equipment to track down Lynn Thomas Fuller of Big Stone Gap, Virginia, in March 1998. Fuller is accused of making more than eight hundred 911 phone calls. Eight hundred! Fuller would only speak to female dispatchers, and when a male dispatcher answered the call, he would hang up. He was released on $1,000 bond. Hopefully, they took away his calling card too!

911 REPORT:

"I got a damn Q-tip stuck in my ear!

CONDOM-NATION

911:   "911."

MAN
(out of breath): "Uh, hey, I feel real stupid about this
                  but . . ."

911:   "Sir, do you have an emergency to
                  report?"

MAN: "You're here to give out information,
                  right?"

911:   "In a way. What's your emergency?"

MAN: "My girl and I are . . . well, you know.
                  About to do it and . . . sh-t . . . I've got
                  a condom here and . . . . Hell, how do
                  you use these things?"

A NEW WATER BED

911 DISPATCHER: "911. Fire or emergency?"

WOMAN: "Yes, I need some help, please."

911 DISPATCHER: "Certainly, ma'am. What's the nature of your emergency?"

WOMAN: "I need you to send a couple of policemen over to 918 Northwood Drive immediately, please."

911 DISPATCHER: "Can you tell me the problem, ma'am?"

WOMAN: "Well, I've been sick . . . uh, very sick . . . for about a week now."

911 DISPATCHER: "Yes, ma'am, and what seems to be the problem?"

WOMAN: "Well, my hot-water bottle broke . . . it just split open and soaked my bed. I would like for you to send a couple of policemen over here and have them flip my mattress. I need to sit down so I'll just leave the door open. Thank you."

911 DISPATCHER: "Hello? Hello?"

DON'T LEAVE HOME WITHOUT IT

Dick Muchow of Phoenix, Arizona, took a wrong step and accidentally broke his ankle. Fortunately, his friend, Doug Steakley, was there. Doug grabbed a cellular phone from Muchow's pack and called 911. So why is this story in a book about weird 911 calls? Because the two men were up 12,700 feet on Lizard Head Peak in Colorado at the time. Several 911 centers received the call since there was little to block the phone's signal. A team of rescuers were sent by helicopter to save the hurt mountaineer and his friend. I hope the two mountaineers hadn't brought a cellular phone on their hike so they could order a pizza.

REPORT ... 911 REPORT ... 911 REP(
. 911 REPORT ... 911 REPORT ... 911
RT ... **911 REPORT ... 911 REPORT .**
. 911 REPORT ... 911 REPORT ... 911
REPORT ... 911 REPORT ... 911 REP(
. 911 REPORT ... 911 REPORT ... 911
REPORT ... 911 REPORT ... 911 REP(
. 911 REPORT ... 911 REPORT ... 911
REPORT "Is it a burn day?" 911 REP(
. 911 REPORT ... 911 REPORT ... 911
REPORT ... 911 REPORT ... 911 REP(
. 911 REPORT ... 911 REPORT ... 911
REPORT ... 911 REPORT ... 911 REP(
. 911 REPORT ... 911 REPORT ... 911
REPORT ... 911 REPORT ... 911 REP(
. 911 REPORT ... 911 REPORT ... 911

REPORT ... 911 REPORT ... 911 REP(

CAT AND MOUSE

911: "911."

CALLER: "Yes, well, I called the vets and they were no help. I was hoping you could."

911: "If I can. What's your emergency?"

CALLER: "My cat, Terrance, caught a mouse. I got the little mouse away before Terrance could kill it. But the silly old cat broke that little mouse's leg."

911: "Ma'am?"

CALLER: "Do you know where I could go to get a cast put on that poor little thing's leg? I'll take care of it until it gets better, don't you worry about that."

THE KING HAS LEFT THE BUILDING

911 DISPATCHER: "911. What's your emergency?"

WOMAN: "Oh, dear God, thank you, thank you. Help . . . please send someone over."

911 DISPATCHER: "Okay, ma'am. Try to stay calm. I need to know what happened."

WOMAN: "Oh, dear God. I'm all right, thank God. I just . . . I just . . ." *(Starts crying.)*

911 DISPATCHER: "Ma'am, do you need an ambulance?"

WOMAN: "No, honey, please send a policeman, or a detective, or someone. My God, I can't believe it. Something like this has never happened to me . . . what's the world coming to?"

911 DISPATCHER: "Ma'am, there's a policeman on the way . . . . Can you tell me what happened?"

WOMAN: "I'll try. I'm sorry . . . it's just that. I'll try. I was sitting watching my show and I hear something in the bedroom. I get up, 'cause I think it Butter, my cat. She gets stuck in the closet sometimes. And I . . . oh, God."

911 DISPATCHER: "It's okay, ma'am."

WOMAN: "There was a man in my bedroom. He was at the bureau drawer and stuffing my things in his pockets. My pills and things. He ran, though, ran scared he did, the moment he saw me. I just can't believe it . . ."

911 DISPATCHER: "Can you describe what the man looked like?"

WOMAN: "Well, he resembles Elvis Presley— but when he was slender, not fat."

IT'S YOUR QUARTER

Six-year-old Steven Varley was trying to keep a quarter away from his eight-year-old brother, Ian. Since Ian was bigger, Steven thought the best place to hide the quarter was in his mouth. So Steven put his money where his mouth is but the quarter had another idea—it slipped down into this throat. Steven's mother, Karen, grabbed the phone and called 911.

"Hi. This is Karen Varley. My six-year-old has a quarter stuck in his throat, lodged in his throat," Varley said.

"Is he able to breathe?" a dispatcher asked.

"A little bit, yes," Varley replied.

The dispatcher gave the mother instructions on how to handle the situation, which she repeated to her son. Paramedics arrived and took Steven to the hospital, where he received an X ray—the doctors received the quarter, and other things, when the boy threw up.

REPORT ... 911 REPORT ... 911 REP
911 REPORT ... 911 REPORT ... 911
REPORT ... 911 REPORT ... 911 REP
911 REPORT ... 911 REPORT ... 911
REPORT ... 911 REPORT ... 911 REP
911 REPORT ... 911 REPORT ... 911
REPORT ... 911 REPORT ... 911 REP

Roger's Department Store
called three times asking
if they should close
during the storm.

911 REPORT ... 911 REPORT ... 911
REPORT ... 911 REPORT ... 911 REP
911 REPORT ... 911 REPORT ... 911
REPORT ... 911 REPORT ... 911 REP
911 REPORT ... 911 REPORT ... 911
REPORT ... 911 REPORT ... 911 REP

REPORT ... 911 REPORT ... 911 REP

LOCAL YOKEL

DISPATCHER: "911. What is your emergency?"

FEMALE CALLER: "Yes, I'm at a pay phone, and I can't get through on a local call."

DISPATCHER: "Ma'am, you have reached 911."

CALLER: "Uh hum. Well . . . I can't make my call."

DISPATCHER: "Ma'am, you have dialed 911. 911 is for emergencies only."

CALLER: "Uh hum. So . . . well, I still can't make my call."

EVERYONE EATS AT DENNY'S

Sheriff's Deputy Charles White of Merritt Island, Florida, thought he had a crank call on his hands when someone called 911 to report that Libyan leader Muammar Gadhafi was eating at a local Denny's. But when White and another deputy walked through the glass door of the restaurant, they quickly spotted Gadhafi eating with a three-year-old boy. It turned out to be thirty-four-year-old Michael Belman and not the dreaded Libyan leader.

"We sat down beside him, and we were just laughing about the whole situation," White said. "He favors him."

Belman, a jeweler from Cocoa, said he's been confused with Muammar many times. "At times it's fun and at times it's fearful," he said. "I've seen [Gadhafi] on TV just a few times. We do favor each other quite a bit." My question to Mr. Belman is—When is it "fun" to look like Muammar Gadhafi?

911 REPORT:

"There is a loud party next door."

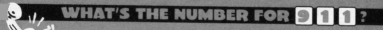

EAT AND GET GAS!

DISPATCHER: "Sheriff's Department."

MALE CALLER: "Yeah, I just ate at [fast food restaurant] and I've been puking my guts out for forty-five minutes. You know, I'm really sick. And I was wondering whether you have gotten any calls from anyone else about anybody gettin' sick from there?"

DISPATCHER: "No sir, we haven't."

CALLER: "OK, well, I was just wondering."

ONLY THE LONELY

DISPATCHER: "Sheriff's Department."

FEMALE CALLER: "Hi, I just got home from a trip and, this is really embarrassing, but somebody left one of those blow-up dolls in my yard. I mean, I can't pick it up and put it in the trash. What are the neighbors going to think when they see me carrying this thing across my yard?"

DISPATCHER: "Couldn't you just let the air out?"

CALL ANY TIME

It's probably the first time a known owner of a call-girl business made a 911 call—but it happened. Dr. Steven Hoefflin, Michael Jackson's plastic surgeon, was walking with a group of people on the Santa Monica Pier after dinner. Hoefflin had never met one of the women in the group, who just happened to be eating at the same trendy restaurant, but he knew of her—Heidi Fleiss, the woman convicted of running a prostitution ring. While the group enjoyed the night air, they suddenly saw a man with his hands cuffed behind his back jump into the water. Hoefflin and another person from the group dove into the 56-degree water and struggled for more than thirty minutes to save the man. Fleiss ran off to do what she does best—she made a phone call. This time it wasn't to any high-profile client. It was to 911 to report the suicide attempt.

REPORT . . . 911 REPORT . . . 911 REPO
911 REPORT . . . 911 REPORT . . . 911
REPORT . . . 911 REPORT . . . 911 REPO
911 REPORT . . . 911 REPORT . . . 911
REPORT . . . 911 REPORT . . . 911 REPO
911 REPORT . . . 911 REPORT . . . 911
REPORT . . . 911 REPORT . . . 911 REPO
911 REPORT . . . 911 REPORT . . . 911

"Is the road over Tehachapi Pass open?"

911 REPORT . . . 911 REPORT . . . 911
REPORT . . . 911 REPORT . . . 911 REPO
911 REPORT . . . 911 REPORT . . . 911
REPORT . . . 911 REPORT . . . 911 REPO
911 REPORT . . . 911 REPORT . . . 911
REPORT . . . 911 REPORT . . . 911 REPO
911 REPORT . . . 911 REPORT . . . 911
REPORT . . . 911 REPORT . . . 911 REPO

MAN-OF-THE-YEAR AWARD

CALLER: "Can you tell me what happened to my girlfriend?"

DISPATCHER: "I will try."

CALLER: "Well, we were having sex. We really started going at it, and she started breathing hard and then passed out at the end. I thought she wasn't breathing so I started doing CPR on her. She came to. She is sleeping now and I think she is fine, but I just wanted to know what happened to her."

DISPATCHER: "Sir, I think it was just *you*. . . . If you want I can send a medic truck over to see if she is OK."

CALLER: "Oh no, she is sleeping now. I think she should be all right in the morning."

THE JOKER'S WILD

Cynthia Divecha of Medina, Ohio, was shocked to see her eighteen-year-old son, John, volunteering to help bring in the groceries from the car. "Call 911. I'm having a heart attack," she said in jest. He did. After he realized his mother was being sarcastic, John recalled 911 to recall the police officer who was already in route—but it was too late.

"I thought he knew I was joking," Divecha said. "But he knows I have been a little stressed lately." Divecha explained the reason for her little joke was that her son usually needs to be forced into doing chores around the house.

"It figures. The first time he actually does something I ask, and it's wrong," Divecha joked. I'll bet she never asks him to do anything else—maybe that was his plan all along.

911 REPORT:

"I was wrestling, and I think I pulled my thumb out of the socket."

FULL OF HOT AIR

911: "911, what's the nature of your emergency?"

WOMAN: "Yes, 911. My cat has floated up to the ceiling, and I can't get her down."

911: "Excuse me, ma'am. Did you say floated?"

WOMAN: "Yes. It's the strangest thing. I know you're going to think I'm crazy."

911: "No, ma'am."

WOMAN: "It's just . . . well, she won't come down, and I don't know how she got up there in the first place."

911: "Is the cat on a shelf or something?"

WOMAN: "No, she's just floating in the air. . . . It's a little scary. Could you please send someone out to help me?"

911: "I can give you the number for the police. 911 is for emergencies only . . . I'm sorry."

WOMAN: "Well, I can't find my glasses. I'm afraid I can't see the numbers of the phone too well—could you dial it for me?"

Police were dispatched to the woman's residence. It turns out the mysterious "floating" cat was actually a helium balloon. The woman's daughter and grandson had visited her earlier that evening, and the young boy accidentally left the balloon behind. Police found the woman's glasses, and her real cat was sleeping soundly on her bed.

SHE'S NICE—
BUT SHE'S NO CHARMER

Lori Rubinfeld, a native of New York City, while visiting a friend in Gainesville, Florida, thought she would live the adage "when in Rome . . . " Showing that a New York girl isn't afraid of anything, Rubinfeld thought she would give her friend's pet python, Snake, a friendly good-morning tickle under the chin. The snake mistook Rubinfeld's fingers for breakfast and sunk its fangs into them while wrapping its five-foot body around her arm.

The python, who had "the weight of a bowling ball," wouldn't let go of Rubinfeld's finger-sandwiches, no matter what his owner, Dan Randall, tried. He suggested putting Rubinfeld's arm and the snake in the freezer— didn't work. Then they tried putting the snake under a running faucet—didn't work, either. Finally, since Rubinfeld's fingers were preoccupied, Randall let his fingers do the walking and called 911.

WHAT'S THE NUMBER FOR 9 1 1 ?

Dispatched firefighters thought long and hard about how to disengage the peckish python. They decided on blasting a carbon dioxide fire extinguisher into Snake's face. After three squeezes of the trigger, the python finally let go and fell to the floor. "I am not a nature girl," Rubinfeld said. "I just think it's so funny that I came down from the Big Bad Apple and this happens. I'm ready to go home now." I'll bet Snake is ready for you to slither away too.

911 REPORT:

"Is this 911?"

ONCE BITTEN . . .

DISPATCHER: "911. What's the nature of your emergency?"

WOMAN: "Yeah, I've been bit by a snake."

DISPATCHER: "Did you say, 'a snake,' ma'am?"

WOMAN: "Yeah, a snake. It bit me on the leg. Is it poisonous?"

DISPATCHER: "How long ago did this happen?"

WOMAN: "A few minutes ago, I don't know. Is the snake poisonous?"

DISPATCHER: "I don't know, ma'am. Where are you?"

WOMAN: "I'm at a 7-11 on . . . on . . . uh, the corner of Fourteenth and . . . " *(Yells to someone)*. . . Madison. Fourteenth and Madison. Was the snake poisonous?!"

DISPATCHER: "I don't have any way of knowing that, ma'am. Just try to stay calm. There's an ambulance on the way."

WOMAN: "It was brown and shiny and had sort of stripes—does that help?"

DISPATCHER: "Ma'am."

WOMAN: "Look, a damn snake bit my leg and all I want to know is, is it poisonous?"

DISPATCHER: "Ma'am, everything is going to be all right. An ambulance will be there in moments. Are you feeling dizzy or nauseous?"

WOMAN: "No, I feel fine. I just want to know if that snake was poisonous. A brown snake, okay. A brown snake with, like, stripes or something—you got it. A brown, striped snake. Now, can you tell me if it's poisonous!!!"

DISPATCHER: "Paramedics will be able to tell you if the snake was poisonous or not."

WOMAN: "Well, that's just great. But I'd sort of like to know now, if you don't mind!"

An ambulance arrived a short while later and the woman was safely taken to the hospital. It was discovered the snake was not poisonous.

CIRCLING THE U

A man entered a U-Gas Mini Mart in High Ridge, Missouri, near St. Louis with the intention of robbing the convenience store. When the holdup man demanded money, the clerk simply refused. This stunned the would-be robber, who left the store in a huff and went back to his car. The clerk called 911, and then followed the man outside to write down his car's license plate number. This bold move apparently peeved the robber, who chased the clerk back into the store and then began driving his car around in circles and screeching his tires. Deputies arrived at the convenience store to find the cruising criminal still circling the parking lot.

911 REPORT:

"I need someone to take my dog to the vet."

WAIT A SPELL

911: "911. Fire or emergency?"

MAN: "Yeah, I heard some gunshots across the street and need someone to come see what's happened."

911: "Is anyone hurt?"

MAN: "How the hell should I know? Like I said, I heard gunshots and now you guys need to come down here and find out what the hell is going on."

911: "What's your address?"

MAN: "1402 West Palimar."

911: "And could I have your name, please?"

MAN: "All right. It's Frank Wymarian."

911: "Sir, could you please spell your name."

MAN (irate): "That's *W* as in *Williams* and *Y* as in *why*."

REPORT ... 911 REPORT ... 911 REP
. 911 REPORT ... 911 REPORT ... 91
RT ... 911 REPORT ... 911 REPORT .
. 911 REPORT ... 911 REPORT ... 91
REPORT ... 911 REPORT ... 911 REP
. 911 REPORT ... 911 REPORT ... 91
REPORT ... 911 REPORT ... 911 REP

"I'm a senior citizen and
I need someone to shovel
my walk, please."

REPORT ... 911 REPORT ... 911 REP
. 911 REPORT ... 911 REPORT ... 911
REPORT ... 911 REPORT ... 911 REP
. 911 REPORT ... 911 REPORT ... 911
REPORT ... 911 REPORT ... 911 REP
. 911 REPORT ... 911 REPORT ... 911

REPORT ... 911 REPORT ... 911 REP

THOSE KIDS WILL DRIVE YOU CRAZY

We all know that most boys like trucks—but one Green Bay, Wisconsin, ten-year-old liked trucks so much he took one on a seventy-five-mile trip. The boy had planned to drive two hundred miles from Keshena to an aunt's house in Milwaukee. But there was a rainstorm and the windshield wipers wouldn't work, so the boy pulled off and called 911. Lt. Roger Lantagne of the Brown County Sheriff's Department was amazed at the young boy's driving skills.

"I asked him how he was able to drive and he said, 'I just moved the seat ahead as far as I could and could reach the pedals,'" said Lantagne. "He said the only thing he didn't like about driving was that his hands got sweaty."

UP THE DOWN STAIRCASE

911: "911. Fire or emergency?"

CALLER: "It's my girlfriend. She's hurt pretty bad."

911: "Where is she hurt, sir?"

CALLER: "Well, I was having a drink, minding my own business, and she started an argument with me. Next thing I know, her ass is falling down the stairs. She hasn't moved so I thought I'd call you guys."

911: "Did she just fall?"

Caller: "No, she just didn't fall . . . I helped her!"

JUDGE NOT, LEST YE BE JUDGED

The court clerk's eyes widened when she read the note handed to her from Judge Claudia Jordan of Denver. The note read: "Blind on the right side. May be falling. Please call someone." Fearing for the health of the judge, the clerk called 911 and requested paramedics to come to the courthouse immediately.

When the clerk told the judge the paramedics were on their way and not to worry, the judge let out a little shriek. She then pointed to the drooping venetian blinds on the right side of the courtroom. "I didn't want anyone to get hurt. I wanted someone from maintenance," Jordan said.

Soon the paramedics arrived, stretcher in tow, and entered the courtroom looking for the ailing judge. Judge Jordan halted a drunk driving case she was hearing to let the emergency team know she was all right and to thank them for their prompt response. I just hope she makes her judgment calls a little more clear than her notes.

911 REPORT . . . 911 REPORT . . . 911 REP
. 911 REPORT . . . 911 REPORT . . . 911
RT . . . 911 REPORT . . . 911 REPORT .
. 911 REPORT . . . 911 REPORT . . . 911
REPORT . . . 911 REPORT . . . 911 REP
. 911 REPORT . . . 911 REPORT . . . 911
REPORT . . . 911 REPORT . . . 911 REP

"Could someone stop
by my house and take me
grocery shopping?"

REPORT . . . 911 REPORT . . . 911 REP
. 911 REPORT . . . 911 REPORT . . . 911
REPORT . . . 911 REPORT . . . 911 REP
. 911 REPORT . . . 911 REPORT . . . 911
REPORT . . . 911 REPORT . . . 911 REP
. 911 REPORT . . . 911 REPORT . . . 911

REPORT . . . 911 REPORT . . . 911 REP

PARTY ON!

DISPATCHER: "911. Please state your emergency."

CALLER: "Yeah, okay. Bill got hurt."

DISPATCHER: "All right, who is Bill?"

CALLER: "Just some dude I know. We were tossing the Nerf around, and the TV fell and cut up his leg . . . like."

911: "We'll send someone right over."

CALLER
(to someone in the room): "Get the keg outta here, dude!"

CRAP OUT OF LUCK

When 911 dispatchers for New York City received a call about a man in trouble, they knew this guy was going to raise a real stink. Paramedics arrived and treated Tim Young of Brooklyn for asphyxiation after he accidentally fell into a filled sewage vat. The man was held under the surface for three minutes before coworkers heard him pounding on the tank. "It's kind of embarrassing when you think about it," said Young. "I mean, here I am passing out under all that mess and I'm thinking to myself: Hey, do I really want to be rescued? If they rescue me, I'll have to explain how I fell in. As it turns out, I guess I did want to be rescued bad enough." When Young was asked by reporters how he happened to fall into the tank—he refused to comment.

911 REPORT:

"My phone doesn't work."

THE MAN WHO CRIED "EUREKA!"

A man from Portland, Oregon, was taken to an emergency clinic after a 911 call for help. The man was suffering from severe bruising and lacerations on his penis and testicles. The cause? A handheld vacuum cleaner. The excuse? He claimed to have been vacuuming wearing only a bathrobe and tripped when the bathrobe fell open. "It always does that," he said. The man fell on the still-whirring vacuum cleaner, and his privates got caught up in the beater bar. As to what he'll do in the future about his errant robe: "I keep meaning to rig up some kind of tie for it, but I never do. I guess I'll get around to it now." The man required fifteen stitches and an overnight stay at the clinic. Boy, don't you just hate it when that happens?

MISS-CONCEPTION

911: "911. What's the nature of your emergency?"

MAN: "My wife is pregnant, and her contractions are only two minutes apart!"

911: "Is this her first child?"

MAN: "No, you idiot! This is her husband!"

REPORT . . . 911 REPORT . . . 911 REP
911 REPORT . . . 911 REPORT . . . 911
REPORT . . . 911 REPORT . . . 911 REP
911 REPORT . . . 911 REPORT . . . 911
REPORT . . . 911 REPORT . . . 911 REP
911 REPORT . . . 911 REPORT . . . 911
REPORT . . . 911 REPORT . . . 911 REP
911 REPORT . . . 911 REPORT . . . 911

"Do you have some
time to just talk?"

REPORT . . . 911 REPORT . . . 911 REP
911 REPORT . . . 911 REPORT . . . 911
REPORT . . . 911 REPORT . . . 911 REP
911 REPORT . . . 911 REPORT . . . 911
REPORT . . . 911 REPORT . . . 911 REP
911 REPORT . . . 911 REPORT . . . 911

REPORT . . . 911 REPORT . . . 911 REP

THE ONE THAT GOT AWAY

A drunken call came into the 911 center in Tacoma, Washington—their friend had fallen into the river. But here's the rest of the story. A group of friends had been drinking and bragging when one of the crew related the story he had heard about someone who bungee-jumped off the Tacoma Narrows Bridge in the middle of the day. The conversation became an "I could do that!" ordeal, and one dare led to another until all ten of the drinkers stormed off to the bridge together, arriving at four-thirty in the morning.

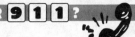

When they got there, they realized no one had brought a bungee cord. Kerry Bingham, who hadn't stopped drinking, was the one who took the dare. He was also the one who spotted a coil of lineman's cable lying nearby. One end of the cable was tied around Bingham's leg, and the other end was secured to the bridge. Bingham crawled on top of the rail and bravely flung himself over the edge.

His cronies watched in amazement as Bingham swan-dived out gracefully toward the icy river below—then the cable yanked taut. Bingham's foot was torn off at the ankle, but the rest of him plunged into the river. He was rescued by two fishermen. "All I can say," said Bingham, "is that God was watching out for me on that night. There's just no other explanation for it." Bingham made a full recovery. His foot, however, was never recovered.

SADDLE UP

911: "911. Fire or emergency?"

CALLER: "This is just the most ridiculous thing. I want the police down here now."

911: "What's the problem, sir?"

CALLER: "I'm a taxpayer and I want the police down here to get rid of these hoodlums that have been coming on my property."

911: "Do you have an emergency, sir?"

CALLER: "Damn straight I do. These three boys jumped my fence . . . I'm watching all this from the upstairs window . . . and, pretty as you please, jump on the back of my sheep and start riding them around my property."

911: "They're riding your sheep?"

CALLER: "Like a damn horse!"

RUN, RUN, AS FAST AS YOU CAN . . .

"Mom, it's the firemen. I told them we have an emergency," said a four-year-old Bazetta, Ohio, boy, during his phone call to 911. Then he added, "and we really do." It was just two weeks before Christmas 1998, and the police who were dispatched to the scene discovered the burning emergency was—the boy's mother had overbaked the gingerbread man. An officer on the scene talked to the boy about the importance of the emergency number.

"He told the boy that because the gingerbread man doesn't breathe and doesn't bleed, there was no need to call 911," Police Chief Robert Jacola said. The scorched gingerbread man and five other cookie "burn victims" were taken to the 911 Center. "We just want to keep them for sentimental value," said dispatcher Roger Laird.

911 REPORT:

"Give me the number for the police. And don't give me any crap about looking up the number myself—I don't have time."

GOING OFF HALF-COCKED

Twenty-one-year-old Darwin Coates was in a cocky mood when he took his .22-caliber pistol and shoved it into the waistband of his pants. He was feeling less cocky (literally) when the gun fired and shot him in the groin. He hobbled to his girlfriend's apartment in Pasadena, Maryland, and called 911. Gregory Johson, a friend of Coates, was also at the apartment. While the two waited for the ambulance, Johson picked up Coates's gun and stuck it in *his* back pocket. The gun went off again and shot Johson in the buttocks. The police arrived and were able to confiscate the gun without shooting themselves.

REPORT . . . 911 REPORT . . . 911 REPO
911 REPORT . . . 911 REPORT . . . 911

REPORT . . . 911 REPORT . . . 911 REPO

911 REPORT . . . 911 REPORT . . . 911
REPORT . . . 911 REPORT . . . 911 REPO
911 REPORT . . . 911 REPORT . . . 911
REPORT . . . 911 REPORT . . . 911 REPO

"Yeah, I need one of you guys
to come out here and help me
push my car out of the snow."

REPORT . . . 911 REPORT . . . 911 REPO
911 REPORT . . . 911 REPORT . . . 911
REPORT . . . 911 REPORT . . . 911 REPO
911 REPORT . . . 911 REPORT . . . 911
REPORT . . . 911 REPORT . . . 911 REPO
911 REPORT . . . 911 REPORT . . . 911

REPORT . . . 911 REPORT . . . 911 REP

I'M SORRY BUT WE'RE NOT IN RIGHT NOW. IF YOU'LL LEAVE A MESSAGE . . .

OPERATOR: "Police, Franklin."

CALLER: "Yeah. Send someone to 65 Stonehedge Drive in Franklin, immediately. There's a young woman there who is not breathing. She's turning blue."

OPERATOR: "65 Stonehenge?"

CALLER: "Stone*hedge*. Hedge, like a bush."

OPERATOR: "OK. In Franklin?"

CALLER: "Yeah."

OPERATOR: "What phone number are you calling from?"

CALLER: "Ah, I don't know. It's a public phone."

OPERATOR: "When were you at that house, sir?"

CALLER: "Bye."

OPERATOR: "Sir?"

SO WHAT'S BUGGIN' YOU?

According to a report in the *Jerusalem Post*, a Tel Aviv man was admitted to a hospital with severe burns, broken ribs, and a broken pelvis—all because of a cockroach. The article explained that the man's wife had become frightened when she saw a large cockroach in her living room. She stepped on the insect—but that didn't kill it. She then picked up the bug, threw it in the toilet, and sprayed an entire can of insecticide into the bowl—which finally did kill the creature.

The woman's husband came home. Knowing nothing about his wife's earlier battle, he went to the bathroom and lit a cigarette. When he threw the cigarette butt into the toilet the insecticide fumes exploded "seriously burning his sensitive parts," the Post reported.

The woman called the emergency number, and paramedics were soon on the scene. They treated the man's wounds and placed him on a stretcher to take him to a local hospital. So how did the man get his pelvis and ribs broken? When the paramedics were told the story of the cockroach, the insecticide, and the cigarette, they laughed so hard they dropped the stretcher down the stairs, breaking the man's pelvis and ribs.

REPORT ... 911 REPORT ... 911 REP
. 911 REPORT ... 911 REPORT ... 91
RT ... 911 REPORT ... 911 REPORT .
. 911 REPORT ... 911 REPORT ... 91
REPORT ... 911 REPORT ... 911 REP
. 911 REPORT ... 911 REPORT ... 91
REPORT ... 911 REPORT ... 911 REP

Female complainant
called to say there was
a stray cat hanging out
in her window well.

. 911 REPORT ... 911 REPORT ... 911
REPORT ... 911 REPORT ... 911 REP
. 911 REPORT ... 911 REPORT ... 911
REPORT ... 911 REPORT ... 911 REP
. 911 REPORT ... 911 REPORT ... 911

REPORT ... 911 REPORT ... 911 REP

SECOND TIME'S A CHARM

Paramedics rushed to the Kentucky home of thirty-two-year-old Phillip Johnson after he called about a gunshot wound. When they arrived, they were told by Johnson that he had purposely shot himself above his left nipple because he wanted to see what it would feel like. The paramedic's report about the December 1996 incident stated that Johnson was "screaming about the pain, over and over." However, on October 2, 1997, another 911 call summoned an ambulance crew to Johnson's house, where the man had once again shot himself with his .22-caliber rifle. Johnson confessed that the December shooting "felt so good," he had to do it again. Well, at least the guy's got a hobby.

911 REPORT:

Very Young Caller: "Do you know Santa Claus's phone number?"

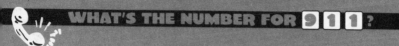

RING AROUND THE DRAIN

911: "911, What's your emergency?"

WOMAN: "I dropped my engagement ring in the toilet, and I don't trust plumbers. Can you please send a policeman to get it out?"

THE VENUS FLY SOFA

Neighbors in Scottsdale, Arizona, were alarmed when they heard frightened but muffled screams coming from their neighbor's house. They called 911, and rescue workers arrived promptly. They entered the house and discovered the woman was inside—trapped in her sleeper sofa. The woman claimed the sofa just snapped shut on her. It took paramedics four hours to remove the woman from her own sofa. I heard of a couch potato before—but this woman almost grew roots.

911 REPORT:

Caller: "We might *(cough)* need the fire department here *(cough)*."

REPORT . . . 911 REPORT . . . 911 REP(
. 911 REPORT . . . 911 REPORT . . . 911
RT . . . 911 REPORT . . . 911 REPORT .
. 911 REPORT . . . 911 REPORT . . . 911
REPORT . . . 911 REPORT . . . 911 REP(
. 911 REPORT . . . 911 REPORT . . . 911
REPORT . . . 911 REPORT . . . 911 REP(
. 911 REDispatcher to police: . . . 911
REPO"Male is sexually stuck to a REP(
. 911 dog and cannot get loose." . . 911
REPORT . . . 911 REPORT . . . 911 REP(
. 911 REPORT . . . 911 REPORT . . . 911
REPORT . . . 911 REPORT . . . 911 REP(
. 911 REPORT . . . 911 REPORT . . . 911
REPORT . . . 911 REPORT . . . 911 REP(
. 911 REPORT . . . 911 REPORT . . . 911
REPORT . . . 911 REPORT . . . 911 REP(

WHERE THERE'S A WILL . . .

In April 1996, Earl Joudrie testified in a Calgary, Alberta, courtroom that his wife, Dorothy, had shot him six times and then pestered him because he didn't die right away. The man testified that after his wife shot him, he pleaded with her to sit next to him, to which she replied, "Well, how long is it going to take you to die?" and "You haven't changed your will, so I'll get everything." After a few minutes, the man stated, Dorothy got a change of heart and called 911. Makes one wonder if the man has changed his will now.

WAKE UP AND SMELL THE COFFEE

DISPATCHER: "911. Fire or emergency?"

MAN: "Yeah, uh, I'm on a business trip, and I know you guys are up early anyway, so . . . "

DISPATCHER: "Sir, do you have an emergency?

MAN: "Well, like I was saying, since you guys are up early in the morning anyway— I was wondering if you could give me a wake-up call."

DISPATCHER: "Excuse me, sir?"

MAN: "A wake-up call. I'm at the Rockford Hotel in room 312. The number is . . ."

DISPATCHER: "I'm sorry, sir. I can't help you unless there is an emergency in progress.

MAN: "Oh. Well. I just thought, you know, you're already awake . . . . What's the big deal!"

(The caller hangs up.)

WORSE THAN THE BUNDY FAMILY

An ambulance crew was dispatched to the Toronto home of Sajid Rhatti after a 911 call about a domestic dispute with injuries was called in. When paramedics arrived, they treated the twenty-three-year-old man for a broken arm and shoulder and various other wounds. The woman suffered from knife wounds to her chest, back, and legs.

The couple had been watching *Married . . . with Children* when they began arguing over who was prettier—Katey Sagal, who plays Peg Bundy, or Christina Applegate, who plays her daughter, Kelly. The argument escalated and the wife slashed Rhatti in the groin with a wine bottle. Things settled down after that: the wife treated her husband's wounds, and they sat down to watch the show again.

Minutes later, the argument flared up again. Rhatti stabbed his wife in the chest, back, and legs and, during the scuffle, suffered a broken arm and shoulder. After the violent episode, they begged neighbors to call 911 for them. Al Bundy would have been proud.

REPORT ... 911 REPORT ... 911 REP
. 911 REPORT ... 911 REPORT ... 91
RT ... 911 REPORT ... 911 REPORT .
. 911 REPORT ... 911 REPORT ... 91
REPORT ... 911 REPORT ... 911 REP
. 911 REPORT ... 911 REPORT ... 91
REPORT ... 911 REPORT ... 911 REP
. 911 REPORT ... 911 REPORT ... 91

"I've got a palmetto bug that
I can't get out of my house."

REPORT ... 911 REPORT ... 911 REP
. 911 REPORT ... 911 REPORT ... 91
REPORT ... 911 REPORT ... 911 REP
. 911 REPORT ... 911 REPORT ... 91
REPORT ... 911 REPORT ... 911 REP
. 911 REPORT ... 911 REPORT ... 911

REPORT ... 911 REPORT ... 911 REP

A DAY WHICH WILL LIVE IN INFAMY

I'm including the following 911 transcript to point out a problem in the system. It doesn't have anything to do with operators or bogus callers. It concerns the actual system itself. In order for 911 operators to dispatch emergency or law enforcement officials, they have to know the exact address—not just a cross street. Here is the infamous 911 phone call about the bomb explosion during the Atlanta Olympics—July 27, 1996. The times have been converted from military to standard times. Punctuation and spelling have been edited. Notes in parentheses are part of the police transcript.

Code 73: Bomb Threat.
Zone 5: A police precinct near Centennial Olympic Park.

12:58:28 A.M.:   [Call to 911]

12:58:32 A.M.:

ATLANTA POLICE DEPARTMENT 911 OPERATOR: "Atlanta 911."

CALLER: "There is a bomb in Centennial Park, you have 30 minutes."

12:58:45 A.M.:   Caller hangs up.

1:01:20 A.M.: 911 operator calls APD Agency Command Center (all lines busy).

1:01:30 A.M.: 911 operator calls Zone 5 and notifies Zone 5 of Signal 73 and requests address of Centennial Park — unable to get street address.

DISPATCHER: "Zone 5."

911 OPERATOR: "You know the address to Centennial Olympic Park?"

DISPATCHER: "Girl, don't ask me to lie to you."

911 OPERATOR: "I tried to call ACC but ain't nobody answering the phone but I just got this man called talking about there's a bomb set to go off in 30 minutes in Centennial Park."

DISPATCHER: "Oh Lord, child. One minute, one minute. I copy Code 17. OK, all DUI units are Code 8 and will not be able to assist on the freeway. Oh Lord, child. Uh, OK, wait a minute, Centennial Park, you put it in and it won't go in?"

911 OPERATOR: "No, unless I'm spelling Centennial wrong. How are we spelling 'Centennial'?"

DISPATCHER: "C-E-N-T-E-N-N-I—how do you spell 'Centennial'?"

911 OPERATOR: "I'm spelling it right, it ain't taking."

DISPATCHER: "Yeah."

911 OPERATOR: "Centennial Park is not going. Maybe if I take 'park' out, maybe that will take. Let me try that."

DISPATCHER: "Wait a minute, that's the regular Olympic Stadium right?"

911 OPERATOR: "Olympic Stadium is like Zone 3, though. Centennial Park."

DISPATCHER: "That's the Centennial Park?"

911 OPERATOR: "It's near the Coca Cola Plaza, I think."

DISPATCHER: "In 5?"

911 OPERATOR: "Uh huh."

DISPATCHER: "Uh, hold on. Sonya, you don't know the address to the Centennial Park?"

2ND DISPATCHER
(in background): "Downtown."

911 OPERATOR: "Male, about 30."

DISPATCHER: "1546, Code 17, 23."

911 OPERATOR: "White."

DISPATCHER: "Uh, you know what? Ask one of the supervisors."

911 OPERATOR: "No, Lord help me, you know they don't know."

DISPATCHER: "I know, but it gets it off you."

911 OPERATOR: "Alrighty then, bye."

DISPATCHER: "Bye."

1:02:40 A.M.: 911 operator calls APD ACC for address (telephone line problem; operators cannot hear each other.)

1:02:50 A.M.: 911 operator calls APD ACC again and requests address for Centennial Park and is given the telephone number.

ACC: "Atlanta Police, Agency Command Center."

911 OPERATOR: "Hey, can you hear me now?"

ACC: "Uh huh."

911 OPERATOR: "OK, can you give me the address of the Centennial Park?"

ACC: "I ain't got no address to Centennial Park, what y'all think I am?"

911 OPERATOR: "Can you help me find the address to Centennial Park?"

ACC: "I can give you the telephone number of Centennial Park."

911 OPERATOR: "I need to get this bomb threat over there to y'all."

ACC: "Well."

911 OPERATOR: "But I need the address of Centennial Park. It's not taking, the system is not taking Centennial Park, that's not where it came from, but you know the system is not taking Centennial Park, that's where he said the bomb was."

ACC: "No particular street or what?"

911 OPERATOR: "He just said there's a bomb set to go off in 30 minutes in Centennial Park."

ACC:	"Ooh, it's going to be gone off by the time we find the address."
911 OPERATOR:	"Are you kiddin'? Give me that, give me that."
ACC:	"I mean I don't have an address, I just have phone numbers."
911 OPERATOR:	"Give me the phone number."
1:05:10 A.M.:	911 operator calls Centennial Park for street address and is placed on hold. Receives address at 1:07:10 A.M.
CENTENNIAL PARK:	"Centennial Park, this is Operator Morgan."
911 OPERATOR:	"Hi, can you give me the address to Centennial Park?"
CEN PARK:	"The address?"
911 OPERATOR:	"Uh huh."
CEN PARK:	"Uh, hold on a second."
1:06:30 A.M.:	911 operator notifies Communications Supervisor, Sgt. Montgomery.

911 OPERATOR: "Does anybody — Sgt. Montgomery, do you know the address of Centennial Park? Do you know the address to Centennial Park? Well, I need to get the address of Centennial Park 'cause, I mean I don't mean to upset nobody, but we got a bomb threat over there."

CEN PARK: "Ma'am."

911 OPERATOR: "Yes."

CEN PARK: "OK, it's 145 International Boulevard."

911 OPERATOR: "145 International Boulevard."

CEN PARK: "Uh huh."

911 OPERATOR: "OK."

CEN PARK: "All right, uh huh."

911 OPERATOR: "Thank you. Bye bye."

1:08:35 A.M.: 911 operator sent call to dispatch.

1:11:10 A.M.:

DISPATCHER: "1591. Radio raising 1594."

UNIT 1594: "1594. You call?"

1:11:20 A.M.:

DISPATCHER: "1594, that's affirmative, got a Signal 73 at 145 International Boulevard. It came from the pay phone at the Days Inn. The caller is advising that he has one set to go off in 30 minutes at Centennial Park. Sounded like a white male."

1:12:30 A.M.:

DISPATCHER: "Did you copy?"

1:12:40 A.M.:

UNIT 1546: "1546. I copy. Advise the state police, they police that park. I'll go the Days Inn and see if I can locate the caller."

DISPATCHER: "OK, that's affirmative."

1:20:00 A.M.:

UNIT 2924: "2924 to Radio, be advised that something just blew up at Olympic Park.

SOURCES

(Albany) *Knickerboker News*

(Allentown) *Morning Call*

Associated Press

Atlanta Journal/Constitution

(Baltimore) *Sun*

Boulder Daily Camera

Bradenton Herald

Calgary Herald

The Canadian Press

Chicago Tribune

Cincinnati Post

(Columbia) *State*

Columbus Dispatch

Columbus Ledger-Enquirer

Dayton Daily News

(Denver) *Rocky Mountain News*

Detroit Free Press

Duluth News Tribune

The Edmonton Journal

Evansville Courier

(Fort Lauderdale) *Sun Sentinel*

Fort Wayne News Sentinel

Fresno Bee

Gary Post Tribune

Grand Forks Herald

Greensboro News and Record

Houston Post

Jackson Citizen Patriot

Kentucky Post

Knoxville News-Sentinel

Lawrence Journal-World

Lexington Herald Leader

Long Beach Press Telegram

(Los Angeles) *Daily News*

Los Angeles Times

Macon Telegraph

(Madison) *Capital Times*

(Madison) *Wisconsin State Journal*

Medina County Gazette

Memphis Commercial Appeal

Miami Herald

(Minneapolis) *Star Tribune*

Myrtle Beach Sun News

(New Jersey) *Record*

New York Newsday

New York Times
(Norfolk) *Ledger-Star*
Orlando Sentinel
Palm Beach Post
(Panama City) *News Herald*
Philadelphia Inquirer
(Phoenix) *Arizona Republic*
Phoenix Gazette
Pittsburgh Post-Gazette
Portland Press Hearld
Reuters
Richmond Times-Dispatch
Roanoke Times and World News
Sacramento Bee
Saint Paul Pioneer Post

St. Louis Post Dispatch
St. Petersburg Times
San Francisco Examiner
San Jose Mercury News
Sault Star
Seattle Post-Intelligencer
Seattle Times
Spokane Spokesman-Review
Tampa Tribune
UPI
USA Today
Vancouver Columbian
Washington Post
Washington Times
York Daily Record